"The worship of God by children is a beautiful moment in the corporate worship experience. If we as ministers, parents, and teachers are to nurture children into faith, we need tools that will equip, support, and enhance that moment. Kelly Belcher's book of sermons offers fresh ideas for the timeless scriptures that flow through the church year. These sermons are filled with creative connections that guide children to offer their presence and praise to God. Most notably, these sermons are held together by the common thread of God's deep love for God's children and the conviction that children need to know that their place in the body of Christ matters."

Ruth Sprayberry DuCharme,
Associate Pastor for Faith Formations for Families,
Highland Hills Baptist Church, Macon, GA

Nurturing Faith in Children

52 Children's Sermons for the Church Year

By Kelly L. Belcher

Carol Brown, Editor

© 2020

Published in the United States by Nurturing Faith Inc., Macon GA,
www.nurturingfaith.net.

Nurturing Faith is the book publishing arm of Good Faith Media (goodfaithmedia.org).

Library of Congress Cataloging-in-Publication Data is available.

ISBN: 978-1-63528-120-0

All rights reserved. Printed in the United States of America.

Scripture quotations are from the New Revised Standard Version Bible, copyright 1989, by the Division of Christian Education of the National Council of Churches in the U.S.A. Used by permission.

Gratitude to Monica Vaughan of Greensboro, N.C., for sponsoring the publication of this volume of children's sermons.

Cover image by David Cassady.

DEDICATION

For my teachers and heroes, Owen and Kera

CONTENTS

Foreword 1

Introduction 3

1) Advent I: Building Hope 5

2) Advent II: Seeking Peace 6

3) Advent III: Finding Joy 8

4) Advent IV: Celebrating Love 10

5) Christmas I: Listening to God 12

6) Epiphany I: Worshiping Jesus 14

7) Epiphany II: Sending Grace and Peace 16

8) Epiphany III: Strong and Unbroken 18

9) Epiphany IV: Called to Follow 19

10) Epiphany V: God's Secret 21

11) Epiphany VI: Growing in God 23

12) Epiphany VII: God as Our Foundation 25

13) Transfiguration Sunday: Changing with Jesus 27

14) Lent I: Power of God's Love 28

15) Lent II: A Hug from Jesus 30

16) Lent III: Second Chances 32

17) Lent IV: A Fierce Love 34

18) Lent V: A Servant Heart 36

19) Palm Sunday: A Humble King 37

20) Easter Sunday: The Best News Ever 39

21) Easter II: Love without Seeing 41

22) Easter III: Love from the Heart 43

23) Easter IV: Help for Our Hurts 45

24) Easter V: Building on Jesus 47

25) Easter VI: Following in Baptism 48

26) Easter VII: Strength through Grace 51

27) Pentecost Sunday: The Spirit Inside Us 53

28) Proper 1/Trinity Sunday: God's Trinity 55

29) Proper 2: A Favorite Present 57

30) Proper 3: Saying No 59

31) Proper 4: Seeking God 61

32) Proper 5: The Beginning and the End 63

33) Proper 6: Bad Days and Good Days 66

34) Proper 7: Doers vs. Hearers 67

35) Proper 8: Paths to Jesus.. 69

36) Proper 9: Hurtful or Helpful Words 71

37) Proper 10: Wise in God's Love 72

38) Proper 11: Power of Prayer 74

39) Proper 12: Picture This!.. 76

40) Proper 13: The Choice for Good... 78

41) Proper 14: Family of God... 80

42) Proper 15: Measuring God's Love... 81

43) Proper 16: Gratitude to God 83

44) Proper 17: Following the Rules 85

45) Proper 18: God's Imagination 86

46) Proper 19: Kids in the Kingdom 88

47) Proper 20: Better than Treasure 90

48) Proper 21: First and Last 92

49) Proper 22/All Saints Day: God's Presence................................. 94

50) Proper 23: Make Your Choice 96

51) Proper 24: All the People.. 97

52) Proper 25/Christ the King: A Gentle King............................... 99

Topical Index 101

Scripture Index 102

FOREWORD

By Kelly L. Belcher

There is nothing more wonderful than participating in the worship of God with children. Their curiosity, receptivity, joy, appreciation and noisy wiggling help us as worshipping adults to stay human; they allow us to embody God more fully.

If you'd like a resource to engage children in weekly worship that welcomes and affirms their questions, furthers their Christian formation, and enables them to become worshippers themselves, then keep reading! You have such a resource in hand.

Helping kids get a handle on the depths of faith is no small job. A recent cartoon showing Jonah inside the belly of the whale, where he was mighty surprised to find Pinocchio, illustrates how confusing the biblical material can be for them.

We may have kids from age 2 to teens in the sanctuary hour. We might have a shifting group with visiting kids as well. It's easy to spend more time just shushing kids than helping them comprehend what worship is, why and who and how we worship, and what is their place before the altar of The Lord God Almighty.

This collection of children's sermons provides ideas and direction for including kids in worship times along with adults. We hope it helps worship leaders help kids participate without making them into a show to entertain adults.

These children's sermons have been compiled and edited from the weekly contributions that were part of the initial Nurturing Faith Bible Studies, giving attention to the cycle of the Church Year.

May these lessons spark the imagination of those who lead children in worship so the children's time is tailored to the leader's personality and the worship setting.

Many thanks to Carol Brown whose editing finesse and experience in shaping the faith of children has brought this collection to its final form. And gratitude to Monica Vaughan of Greensboro, N.C., for sponsoring this volume.

May this Sunday-by-Sunday journey of faith help all of us to sit for a while on Jesus' knee.

INTRODUCTION

God calls us to love everyone as beloved children of God. To love someone we must desire to understand them, to listen to them, and to pay attention to them. This includes the youngest among us—the children in our congregations. If we hope to encourage children to develop a personal faith in God, we must first love them. Loving children means paying attention to children. It means thinking about their experiences and trying to see the world through their eyes.

As we gather as a congregation of believers to worship God each Sunday, our children are watching and listening. By providing a time to tell the stories of God in a way that the children can understand, we are demonstrating to the children that they are important to God. We are saying that God loves them and desires their worship as much as the worship of the adults. The children's sermons that we share during this set-aside time should draw children into the rhythm of worship and help them connect to God in a deeper way. By focusing on the scripture passage or sermon theme of the day, the children's sermon can illustrate the scripture for the children and enhance the worship experience for adults and children alike.

From the first Sunday of Advent to Christ the King Sunday (the end of the church year), the church year seasons reflect the rhythm and seasons of our lives. Following the movement of the church year and choosing scriptures and themes from the lectionary will broaden our worship services to include texts that we would often not choose on our own. When our children are included in these same church year themes, we can expose them to many rich stories, scriptures, and biblical characters that they might not discover through the typical Sunday school lessons and stories.

In this book, you will find 52 children's sermons—one sermon for each Sunday in the church year. Each sermon is based on a focus passage, with a short portion of the passage noted as a memory verse. The author has provided a bit of background to summarize the focus of each children's sermon. Most of the children's sermons presented in the book include objects or props to help bring the words to life for the children. The props are included in the "Items for Preparation" list before each sermon. Each children's sermon concludes with a prayer, which is usually an opportunity for the children to repeat the simple prayer as the leader says each line. Children learn religious practices through modeling and practice—your prayers can introduce young hearts to the language of prayer.

Let these sermons serve as a guide. Adapt them as you see fit so that your group of children will grasp their meaning and grow in their understanding of spiritual themes. As you spend time with children in worship, count it a privilege to convey to your children a love of scripture, a passion for learning, a desire to know the heart of God, and a love for the wonderful stories of the Bible.

1) ADVENT I

Building Hope

Focus Passage: Isaiah 2:1–5

Memory Verse: "…neither shall they learn war any more." (Isaiah 2:4)

Items for Preparation:
- choose one Christmas carol for the season of Advent and sing one stanza each week at the end of the children's sermon
- small ball of play dough, about the size of a walnut, for each child; place play dough in zip-top bags
- photo of a spear or a bow and arrow
- photo of a plow pulled by animals
- hand trowel, shovel, rake, or hoe

Background: This is the Advent day of hope, and we want to focus on what we hope for, and what is in our power to create, by hearing these words of Isaiah. It can be difficult for young children to find meaning in these metaphors, especially when they know nothing of a contemporary agrarian life, much less an ancient one. Focus on tools, and words, that can be used for either good or bad.

Children's Sermon:

[Give a zip-top bag of play dough to each child, so they can open it and begin forming a shape as you talk.]

> **Say:** Today is the Advent Sunday of hope. The prophet Isaiah wrote about a time he hoped for, when life would be good for all the people of Israel. He described it, saying that people could take the things they used as weapons, like swords and knives, meant to hurt one another, and instead could change them into tools, things meant to create and build a life together. You can see some things I have here—some are tools, and some are weapons. And *some* things can be used both ways, can't they? What do you think about these things I have here? How are they used? [Allow for answers and comments. Explain each item so kids will know what it is possibly used for.]
>
> **Say:** Today we have big machines—plows, combines, and big trucks—that can do a lot of farm work in a short time. But in Isaiah's time, a person had to walk, pulling a plowshare along the ground so the dirt could be opened

up and seeds could be planted. If a farmer had enough money, he could buy animals to pull the plowshare for him. It was very hard work. When you work in your garden, you probably use a hoe, or shovel, or hand trowel to move dirt so you can plant seeds. These tools are very small versions of the plowshare that Isaiah was talking about.

Say: What Isaiah wanted us to know is that we have a chance to use tools either to hurt each other or to help one another. Isaiah said that God intended for us to live peacefully, and to make life good for each other. You have a piece of play dough and can choose to make anything with it. You can make something that will be hurtful, or mean, or that will cause someone to feel bad. You can also make something that could help somebody, or make somebody feel good, or make someone feel loved. Now that you've heard Isaiah's words, what will you make? What will you shape your play dough to become? What do you hope might happen?

Pray: Each week, we will sing a verse of a Christmas carol as our prayer to God. Let's sing the first verse now as a prayer.

2) ADVENT II

Seeking Peace

Focus Passage: Isaiah 11:1–10

Memory Verse: "They will not hurt or destroy on all my holy mountain." (Isaiah 11:9)

Items for Preparation:
- choose one Christmas carol for the month of December and sing one stanza each week at the end of the children's sermon
- green construction paper, cut into olive leaf shapes, one for each child; write "forgiven" on each leaf
- copy of Edward Hicks' *Peaceable Kingdom* painting, found here: https://en.wikipedia.org/wiki/Edward_Hicks#/media/File:Edward_Hicks_-_Peaceable_Kingdom.jpg

Background: Today is the Advent Sunday of peace, and we hope to help children learn how to bring peace to themselves and to others with the tool of forgiveness.

Children's Sermon:
[Display your *Peaceable Kingdom* print.]

> **Say:** Today is the Advent Sunday of peace. What do you think we mean when we say the word, "peace"?

[Allow for answers. Try to generate an understanding that runs the gamut from "not bothering my brother" to "no war between any countries on earth" and things in between.]

> **Say:** A famous artist named Edward Hicks painted this picture, which makes us think of the words we hear from the prophet Isaiah today. Isaiah said that animals who usually would chase and eat each other would instead relax together safely. Which animals do you see in this painting? Which ones do you think might not really be safe close to each other? Do you see the babies at the bottom? The one on the lion's back? Can you see a leopard? A tiger? A wolf? A lamb? Would they usually get along okay together? No way! Just like dogs and cats, these animals would be chasing each other all over the place. Those babies would not be safe, would they?

> **Say:** Isaiah wrote about the kind of peace that Edward Hicks painted here, where ones who usually would fight or hurt each other stopped, and were calm and peaceful together. Isaiah wrote that God said, "They will not hurt or destroy in all my holy mountain," and meant that each one would act in a peaceful way toward the others.

> **Say:** What about people? Do you think people can be part of this picture? Do you think Isaiah also meant that God wanted people to be peaceful together?

[Allow for answers.]

> **Say:** I'm giving each of you an Advent present, a handy tool you can use to help bring a peaceful time like Isaiah described. An old symbol or sign that people wanted to be peaceful was an olive branch. I'm giving you just one "olive leaf" that you can use to help make Isaiah's words true today. Your leaf says "forgiven" on it. [Hand out the leaves.]

> **Say:** Now think hard about what Isaiah wrote, and think about this painting, and the animals in it. Now imagine that you are in the painting, together with a person you really do not like. Don't name any names! Sshh. Picture yourself

in the painting, with a person you would want to chase down and fight, or a person who has been mean to you, or a person you have treated badly yourself. Picture yourself next to the person you are most afraid would chase you down and fight with you. Use your olive leaf, with the word "forgiven" on it, and give it to that person. Just picture doing that. Close your eyes if you have to, and see yourself giving the olive leaf to that mean person. Maybe you can really give your olive leaf away for real this week, and celebrate the Advent of peace.

Pray: Each week, we are singing a verse of a Christmas carol as our prayer to God. Let's sing the second verse now as a prayer.

3) ADVENT III

Finding Joy

Focus Passage: Isaiah 35:1–10

Memory Verse: "The desert shall rejoice and blossom." (Isaiah 35:1)

Items for Preparation:
- choose one Christmas carol for the month of December and sing one stanza each week at the end of the children's sermon
- white board, tablet, or pad of paper on which you can write as children dictate

Background: Isaiah's words here are so full of imagery, and so replete with metaphor, that we must narrow our focus to one idea—that what is dry will come to life and be made fresh again. Since Isaiah wrote poetry, children can write their own poetry after the manner of Isaiah to illustrate for themselves their understanding of this idea.

Children's Sermon:
[Read again Isaiah 35:1, 4a, 5, 6b, and 10. Talk through these verses with your group of children so they understand the ideas presented.]

Say: Today is the Advent Sunday of joy, and Isaiah writes for us a very happy and joyful poem. I wonder if we can do the same thing Isaiah did, and write about the way God brings joy and freshness to us. I need your help.

[Pick up your white board or tablet and sit among children so they can see it.]

Say: Isaiah wrote about a time when people lived outdoors much more than we do now. Some lived in tents and moved from place to place. Some lived near a river so they could get water; some lived in mountains, where they could be dry and safe. Isaiah's poem has a lot of outdoor ideas. Since we live inside houses, we could write a new poem about the ways God makes our lives fresh. I'll write down what you say, and you tell me what to write.

Say: First, name a time in the past week when you were not feeling happy, when you were sad, or disappointed, or angry, or hurt. What was happening to you that made you feel that way?

[Allow responses. Re-phrase what children say to apply to all children. For example, if a child says, "I got a bad grade on my test," you could write "The tests at school were too tough for us," or "Even though I studied hard, my answers were wrong."

Write several lines as children give their responses. As you are writing, leave room to add a sentence between each of these phrases. Stop when you get four or five ideas written.]

Say: Wow. We have a lot of troubles every day, don't we? There is a lot happening that is hard for us. Who can give us the help that we need? What can we do when we are feeling this way? What would Isaiah say?

[Allow for responses.]

Say: Isaiah would say to trust in God and God's love for us, and to pray that God will work in us to make something new happen. Let's think again about what we wrote, and write something we hope could happen with God's help.

[Take each idea in order, one by one, and apply what you hear children saying they hope for, phrasing it and writing it as a couplet line in your "poem." Don't worry! Real poems don't have to rhyme! Under the line we mentioned above about hard tests, the response could be something like, "But God gives me wisdom to understand and learn." After you move through each of your four or five ideas, you'll have an eight-to-ten line "poem" which is very like what Isaiah has written in chapter 35.]

Say: Okay! Let's read our Isaiah-ish poem, and see if we have the idea Isaiah was trying to tell us.

[Read your new "poem" aloud. End it with the last lines of Isaiah's chapter, Isaiah 35:10b.]

Say: Just like God was with Isaiah, God is here with us, and God will help us bring joy out of trouble.

Pray: Each week, we have been singing a verse of a Christmas carol as our prayer to God. Let's sing the third verse now as a prayer.

4) ADVENT IV

Celebrating Love

Focus Passage: Isaiah 7:10–17

Memory Verse: "The Lord himself will give you a sign." (Isaiah 7:14)

Items for Preparation:
- choose one Christmas carol for the month of December and sing one stanza each week at the end of the children's sermon
- crèche or nativity scene with characters

Background: Today is the Advent Sunday of love. Our children's sermon is a simple Christmas lesson, but important especially for small children, who need to hear and see it again and again as they grow.

Children's Sermon:
[Display the crèche or nativity]

Say: Today is the Advent Sunday of love, the last Sunday before…what?

[Allow answers and lots of excitement!]

Say: Yep, it's almost Christmas Eve. And you know what that means! What happens on Christmas Eve?

[Allow answers. Most of them will have to do with Santa and that's okay.]

Say: Yes, on Christmas Eve we know what to expect. And how do you know that Christmas is coming in just a couple of days? What tells you we are getting close to Christmas? What are the signs?

[Allow for answers—decorations, gift-buying and wrapping, cooking, parties, worship services, etc.]

Say: You are naming all the signs that Christmas is coming. Even somebody who had never celebrated Christmas before would be able to tell it was coming by seeing all these signs of Christmas around us. But do you know that there wasn't always a Christmas? There was a time over 2000 years ago when there was *no such thing* as Christmas! Can you imagine?

Say: But a little over 2700 years ago, there was a King of Judah named Ahaz. Isaiah writes that the Lord spoke to Ahaz, and told him what was going to happen. It wasn't at all what Ahaz was expecting to hear.

Say: The Lord told King Ahaz that a young woman would have a little baby, and name him "Emmanuel." That Hebrew name is really two words that mean, "God is with us." What is the name you know for the baby in the manger who was born on Christmas Eve?

Say: Before Jesus was born, the people believed that a great king was coming. They expected the new king to be royal, to live in a palace, to have a mighty army and lots of riches, and be powerful. But look again at the little baby in the manger. Does he look like the kind of king Isaiah's people were expecting? Nope. He's very different. But the Lord told King Ahaz that the new baby would be a sign that God is with us. We call him Jesus, Emmanuel, Lord, Savior, and Prince of Peace. We celebrate his birthday really well on Christmas Day. The Lord is with us, and Jesus' birth is the sign that the Lord will always be with us forever.

Pray: Each week, we have been singing a verse of a Christmas carol as our prayer to God. Let's sing the fourth verse now as a prayer.

5) CHRISTMAS I

Listening to God

Focus Passage: Matthew 2:13–23

Memory Verse: "An angel of the Lord appeared to Joseph in a dream." (Matthew 2:13)

Items for Preparation:
- choose one Christmas carol for the month of December and sing one stanza each week at the end of the children's sermon
- pillow, blanket, sleep mask; maybe even wear flannel pajamas
- nametag with "Joseph" in large print
- recruit a volunteer to play Joseph, if you prefer

Background: We'll tell the story of Jesus' escape from Herod, but focus, not on the deaths of children, but on the whisper of God into the ear of Joseph, helping him to protect Jesus.

Children's Sermon:
[Have your sleeping gear donned, and have on your "Joseph" nametag. Lie down on the nearest pew, settle into your pillow, pull your sleep mask over your eyes, yawn, stretch, and pull those covers up over you. Hunker down. Let kids laugh at you while you do it. Breathe heavier. Begin to snore. Ham it up. Now, pretend to hear something, and get startled awake. Open your eyes, look around, and sit bolt upright, looking all around you.]

> **Say:** I was sure I heard something. It must have been a dream. Hey! Do you hear a baby crying? Listen! [Stay quiet a minute, looking around, and hear nothing.]
>
> **Say:** That's good. Baby Jesus cries at night sometimes, and Mary has to give him a drink of milk to get him to settle down and go back to sleep. But I don't hear him crying tonight. He must be sound asleep. I think Mary is asleep, too. Boy, am I sleepy!

[Yawn and stretch again, and prepare to settle back down, and then pause, and listen, and hit your forehead with the heel of your hand as if you have just realized something important.]

Say: Ah! Now I remember why I woke up! It wasn't because baby Jesus was crying. It was because of the dream I had. I dreamed that God was whispering into my ear. God was telling me that we needed to leave right away. God told me to pack up and go to the land of Egypt. What a dream! And I wonder why I dreamed that? Just yesterday, three kings arrived on beautiful camels, wearing rich fine clothes and jeweled crowns. You should see the presents they brought to our new baby! I have no idea why three important and powerful kings would visit our new baby. And the presents! Gold, frankincense, myrrh, and lots of baby toys.

Say: But this dream I just had, it was God whispering to me that I need to protect baby Jesus from a king. There is another king coming to visit him, and this king is not friendly. He is not going to bring presents. He wants to take baby Jesus away. Oh no!

[Begin to get moving. Sit up, straighten your blanket, take off your sleep mask and get yourself together. Fold up your stuff, and "pack" it into a nice neat pile, ready for traveling. As you are doing this, finish your narrative.]

Say: I think God was really speaking to me in that dream. I don't know how or why, but I know what I have to do to keep our baby safe. Mary and I have to pack up and take Jesus away tonight. We can't wait until morning. We need to go now! We need to go all the way across the border and into Egypt. Then, we'll be safe. In Egypt, a whole different country, the king can't get to us. Surely, if I obey God, God will be with us as we travel. Good thing that dream woke me up! I have to do it right now!

[Now pick up your pile of things, and pretend to yell across the room.]

Say: Oh, Mary! Wake up! Get the baby! We're leaving tonight!

Pray: Each week, we have been singing a verse of a Christmas carol as our prayer to God. Let's sing the first verse again as our final December prayer.

6) EPIPHANY I

Worshiping Jesus

Focus Passage: Matthew 2:1–12

Memory Verse: "Opening their treasure chests, they offered him gifts of gold, frankincense, and myrrh." (Matthew 2:11)

Items for Preparation:
- box wrapped in birthday paper with bow
- add gift tag on package with "To Baby Jesus, From ???"

Background: Today the church feast day of Epiphany is celebrated. This day marks the presentation of Jesus in the temple to Simeon and Anna in one gospel story, and the trip of the magi bearing gifts in another. A good definition for the word "epiphany" is "something that was a secret is revealed." Children may be familiar with Matthew's story of the magi, who were probably scientists, astrologers, and consultants to the king's court.

Children's Sermon:

[Place your wrapped gift where all can see it easily.]

Say: Merry Christmas and Happy New Year! Today is Epiphany Sunday, when we celebrate the new baby Jesus and the people who came to meet him. When a new baby is born, friends and family usually come by and visit, to get a chance to hold the new baby and see how happy his parents are. Have you ever visited a family with a new baby, or have you had a new baby in your family before?

[Allow for answers.]

Say: People sometimes bring something with them when they visit the new baby…what do they bring?

[Allow for answers.]

Say: People sometimes bring some food for the baby's family, and they usually bring a present for the baby, because the baby is brand new and doesn't have any stuff yet! He or she needs clothes, and toys, and blankets, and diapers, and lots of other things so he or she can be comfortable, right? What presents have you taken to new babies?

[Allow for answers.]

Say: Matthew tells us the story of when Jesus was a brand new baby. Probably lots of people came to visit Jesus who were friends of his parents, Mary and Joseph. But this story tells of some wise visitors who were important people to King Herod; they were called "magi," which means they were very smart and the king probably went to them when he needed advice. They were his helpers. The king sent them to see where baby Jesus was and to take very fine gifts. What presents did they take to baby Jesus?

[Allow for answers.]

Say: That's right—they did not take diapers, or onesies, or bottles and pacifiers, or blankets and teddy bears—none of the usual stuff people take as presents for new babies! No, they took gold, which was fine and precious, frankincense, which was a spice that smelled very good. And they took myrrh, which was a very strong smelling spice that was used to bury people. These are very funny presents for a new baby!

[Now point to your wrapped gift.]

Say: And this is a gift for baby Jesus, too. On Epiphany, this is a gift for Jesus to worship him and to celebrate his being born. What do you think is in this present? What could we bring to Jesus that he would most like us to bring?

[Allow for answers.]

Say: Maybe Jesus would like some sharing—can you give that? Can you give being obedient to your parents and teachers? Can you give trying your hardest? Can you give him your worship?

Say: On Epiphany day, which is the 12th day of Christmas, think of what you could bring as a gift to Jesus. What would Jesus want most from you? How could your present show Jesus that you love him very much?

[Be sure to leave the unopened gift near the altar following your children's sermon.]

Pray: Say these words after I say them.

> O God of Christmas,
> Accept the gifts we bring
> To show our love for Jesus.
> Let us keep giving all year long
> To you and to each other,
> In Jesus' name, Amen.

7) EPIPHANY II

Sending Grace and Peace

Focus Passage: 1 Corinthians 1:1–9

Memory Verse: "Grace to you and peace…" (1 Corinthians 1:3)

Items for Preparation:
- notecards, pencils, or pens for each child
- a few adult helpers to position four or five older children around your sanctuary

Background: Paul communicated with the new churches through letters. Children may not be familiar with written letters, except maybe thank you notes for birthday gifts. Since writers of biblical material had no idea we'd be communicating electronically now, we must help children of our current age understand what it was like for them to communicate by hand-delivered post.

Children's Sermon:
[Hand a notecard and pen or pencil to every child as you begin.]

> **Say:** There is a special kind of writing that starts out like this: "Dear Friend, Hello! I hope you are doing well, and things are going great for you!" Have you seen writing like that before? What is that called?

[Allow for answers.]

> **Say:** Yes, this is a letter. Maybe you've written letters and mailed them to people, or sent a birthday card or thank you card. Or maybe you write emails and send them to your grandmother. How do you send a message to someone far away? How did people send messages to other people far away in the years when Paul lived, in the first century AD? You guessed it! They wrote letters. There was no Facebook, no email, no phones, no computers, no other way of getting a message to someone except to write it down and send it to them. Paul wrote a lot of letters, because he traveled to many cities to visit people and tell them about Jesus. The verses we read today are part of his letter to a city called Corinth.

[Ask the four or five selected children to stand up, and position each of them around your sanctuary so they are too far apart to be able to talk to each other—at least several pews between them. Use your helpers as needed.]

Say: Now I'm going to pretend that I am Paul, and I'm going to give a very important message to (*name of the child nearest to you*). What I hope is that (*name of child*) will send my message on to (*name of next child closest to you*) and he or she will send it on to the next person, and so on, until every person has the message.

[Walk over to the first child, and whisper into his or her ear the following secret message.]

Whisper: "Please write on your letter the words 'Grace to you and peace.' After you write the message, fold your notecard and tiptoe over to (*name of the next child*) and give your note to him or her. In a whisper voice, ask him or her to write the same note on their notecard and take it to the next child."

Say: Okay, now my message is getting passed on to each one of you. Let's see if they understood the message. What did your message say?

[What we hope is that all the kids will be able to say, "Grace to you and peace!" Invite the children to come back to sit with the other children as you continue.]

Say: This is exactly what Paul did. He wrote his letters to the far-away cities he had visited, telling the people he had met how to be Jesus-followers. And they passed on the messages of grace and peace he gave them. We can read some of them right now, in the Bible, just as if they were written to us.

Pray: Say these words after I say them.

> O loving God,
> We ask that you will use us
> As messengers
> To pass along your words
> Of grace and peace in the world,
> In Jesus' name, Amen.

8) EPIPHANY III

Strong and Unbroken

Focus Passage: 1 Corinthians 1:10–17

Memory Verse: "…that all of you be in agreement and that there be no divisions among you." (1 Corinthians 1:10)

Items for Preparation:
- thread in several different colors
- lengths of about 18 inches from each color, making two different color threads for each child

Background: We never hear the lesson of indivisibility enough. If you have some sets of brothers and sisters among your group of children, have them sitting front and center.

Children's Sermon:

[Hold up your cords of thread, and pass them out so each child has two threads in different colors. Hold up one of your two threads as you talk.]

> **Say:** You heard the verses we read from Paul's letter to Corinth. It makes me think that he wrote this part of his letter because there were some people in the church who did not agree with each other. It could be that they were in an argument with each other. Has that happened to you? Or it could be they disagreed about what Paul had tried to teach them. Or it could be that they were just the kind of people who didn't like each other already, and they used Paul's teaching as one more way not to like each other. Has that happened to you?

> **Say:** Paul wrote some important words to the people he loved in Corinth. He asked them to agree with each other, to be agreeable, and not to let themselves be separate, or take different sides.

> **Say:** It's sort of like the thread you have in your hand. You have two threads. Pick up one of them, and see if you can break it. Try hard.

[Snap one of your threads as you talk, to demonstrate. You can bite it if you have to.]

Say: It's pretty easy to tear apart one little thread. But maybe it's not so easy to tear apart many who join together. Let's try that. Everybody take the thread you have left, and let's put them together.

[Let each child hand you his or her thread, and hold them together in a bundle. Twist them together a little when you get them all.]

Say: Now, can you break this one? Who would like to try?

[Hold fast to your end of the twisted cord of threads, and let kids try to tear it, within reason.]

Say: This is the message Paul was writing. He hoped that the friends in Corinth would agree with each other, be on the same side with one another, and be strong Jesus-followers together, unbroken, and very strong.

Pray: Say these words after I say them.

> O mighty God,
> We are weak, but you are strong.
> Let us be one
> With each other and with You,
> In Jesus' name, Amen.

9) EPIPHANY IV

Called to Follow

Focus Passage: 1 Corinthians 1:18–31

Memory Verse: "God's foolishness is wiser than human wisdom." (1 Corinthians 1:25)

Items for Preparation:
- ask the pastor or preacher to stand before the children as your "example"
- discuss the interview questions with the pastor ahead of time

Background: We will focus on the idea of calling. We will use the preacher as a prime example of a person who answers a calling to serve God, to be wise and strong, to spend time for a sacred purpose, to be alongside Christians as they envision their identity, mission and corporate calling, and to accomplish the ritual sacramental observances that are important to us as God's children, which help us feel our own calling.

Children's Sermon:

Say: Paul wrote a letter to the people in the new church group in the city of Corinth, helping them understand how to be good Jesus-followers. They were just starting out being Jesus-followers in a world that did not know Jesus like we do. In this part of Paul's letter, he is writing about something you and I have both felt, which the people who lived in Corinth felt too. Some of them felt like they weren't good enough to be Jesus-followers. Have you ever felt that way, that you weren't good enough? You don't have to raise your hand, but maybe you have felt like other people were thinking that you were not very smart, or good enough to be part of the group, or enough like them to be one of them.

Say: We ALL have felt this way.

Say: This is the reason that Paul wrote this part of his letter to the city of Corinth. He wanted us to understand something new and wonderful about Jesus. He wrote that Jesus is the "smartness" we all need. Jesus is the strength we need. As long as we believe in Jesus and want to follow him, we are good enough. Jesus makes us good enough. It is good enough for us to decide to be Jesus-followers. There is no way to be "not good enough" or to be "too good" to follow Jesus. This is because we are "called" to follow Jesus. Who knows what that means?

[Allow for answers.]

Say: I know somebody who is handy and nearby who understands exactly what it means to be "called" the way Paul is talking about.

[Ask your pastor, preacher, or minister to stand up or sit with children, as you interview that person.]

Say: You know what we mean when we talk about calling, right? What would you say it means when we talk about people being "called"?

[The pastor can answer in her or his own words; ask any of the following interview questions and allow your pastor to answer.]

Say: Does it mean that God's Spirit makes you feel a certain way? Does it mean that you feel like you almost just can't help it, but you need to do a certain thing to obey God? Does it mean that you feel like you are meant to be or do something wonderful for Jesus' sake? Does being called mean you are better, smarter, stronger or more holy than other people? Can anybody be called, or just ministers? How can you tell that you are called? What are some of the jobs people do when they are "called"?

Say: What Paul wrote to the church people in Corinth was that, when Jesus calls us to follow him, we don't have to worry that we aren't good enough to do what Jesus wants us to do. God will help us know how to answer Jesus' calling. God always helps us do what God is hoping we will do. What a big relief! Maybe when you are a grown-up, God will call you to become a pastor like (*name of your pastor*). Who knows what calling God is planning for all of you. That is an exciting idea.

Pray: Say these words after I say them.

> O mighty God,
> Let us be wise and strong
> So we may follow Jesus
> And answer you when you call
> That we might serve you as Paul did,
> In Jesus' name, Amen.

10) EPIPHANY V

God's Secret

Focus Passage: 1 Corinthians 2:1–16

Memory Verse: "No eye has seen, nor ear heard…what God has prepared for those who love him." (1 Corinthians 2:9)

Items for Preparation:
- giant party eyeglasses or googly-eye glasses or Groucho Marx glasses
- magnifying glass or spyglass

Background: We will build on what we taught last week about calling by focusing on the idea of the "secret" that God has in store for us as Jesus-followers. Our focus is on the feeling of excitement and happiness we have when we imagine what God plans for us, and what the Holy Spirit gives to us that we don't know about yet. This includes our future lives and our eternal life to come.

Children's Sermon:

[Put on your goofy glasses, or take out your spyglass or magnifying glass and put it in front of your eye and look around]

Say: I'm so excited!

[Take a few exaggerated steps back and forth, up and down, with your prop.]

Say: I am just so excited! Are you excited? You should be excited! This is very exciting! My goodness, did you hear Paul's letter this morning? Did you hear the part where it says the exciting stuff?

Say: Well, Paul wrote in his letter to Corinth that "no eye has seen" the wonderful thing that God is getting ready for us. I mean, even with THESE GLASSES, I just can't see it yet. I am trying. I know it is here somewhere! No eye has seen it yet! But I'm working on it! Paul also wrote "no ear has heard" the sound of this wonderful thing that God has for us. What do you think that will sound like? I just can't imagine! I can think of a lot of stuff that sounds wonderful. Popcorn popping. Ocean waves crashing. Ballgames starting. Friends laughing. Paul wrote that the sound of this thing will be even better than that. NO ear has heard it before. Wow!

Say: Paul wrote that this wonderful, exciting thing that God is getting ready for us is going to be brought to us by the Holy Spirit. Hmm, that makes me get even more excited. Do you know who the Holy Spirit is?

[Allow for answers.]

Say: That's right; the Holy Spirit is a part of God. There are three parts of God. One part of God is the part that makes everything in creation. We call God "Creator" because of the stuff God makes.

Say: And God also was inside Jesus, who we call Messiah, the Redeemer and Savior. Jesus is God's son, in a special way all by himself. Jesus is the Christ, the part of God that saves us. That's two parts of God. The third part of God is Spirit.

[Use those glasses, or that spyglass, and look around like you are hunting for something.]

Say: The Holy Spirit isn't something we can see, even with THESE glasses. But the Spirit is here. The Spirit is in you and me and all around us, giving us a feeling of excitement that there are good things ahead. The Spirit gives us strength to do hard things really well. The Spirit gives us ideas, and gives us the feeling that God is close to us. The Spirit gives us comfort and relief when we are afraid, worried, hurt, or ashamed. The Holy Spirit is the third part of God.

Say: So now you know why I am excited: it is because of what Paul wrote. Paul wrote that no eye has seen, and no ear has heard, the wonderful thing that God is getting ready for us, and the Holy Spirit will *bring* it to us. So we all can be excited. There is something very good coming to us. The Holy Spirit is close to us, giving us good things from God. You better start looking around! What will the Holy Spirit bring?

Pray: Say these words after I say them.

> O refreshing God,
> Keep our eyes open
> Keep our ears listening out
> For the surprise of your Holy Spirit
> So we can find what you make for us
> In Jesus' name, Amen.

11) EPIPHANY VI

Growing in God

Focus Passage: 1 Corinthians 3:1–9

Memory Verse: "For we are God's servants, working together." (1 Corinthians 3:9)

Items for Preparation:
- enlist the assistance of a mother who will bring her baby into worship, sitting with your children so they can see the baby well
- option 2: baby-sized doll in a blanket

Background: Our focus is on understanding that we keep growing as Jesus-followers. We start out knowing nothing, and learn bit-by-bit, day-by-day, one experience at a time, how to follow Jesus, and how to be the people God creates us to be. We will aim to show children directly how understanding of God grows in each of us.

Children's Sermon:
[Have the mom sit beside the children, holding her baby so they can get a good look. If she's willing, let children hold the baby's hand, touch her head, wiggle her toes, etc. If you have a doll, hold the "baby" close in a loving way so children will get the idea that babies are loved and cared for completely.]

>**Say:** Shhhh…let's be a little quiet, and be careful and gentle around the baby. We want her to be comfortable and relaxed with us. Have you had a new baby in your house? What are new babies like?

[Allow for answers.]

>**Say:** Some of you might know a lot about what happens when a baby is around. Babies can't do anything themselves, can they? This baby doesn't even know my name, or the name of our church building, or the name of our city, does she?

>**Say:** This baby can't get her own food or milk. She does not know how to get into bed by herself to go to sleep. She can't pull up her own blanket to stay warm. She needs somebody's help for everything, doesn't she?

>**Say:** What about how she knows who loves her. How does she know that?

[Allow for answers.]

>**Say:** She can tell by the way her mom hugs her that her mom loves her, and her dad, and the people who hold her and take care of her. She can tell by the gentleness in the way they touch her that she is safe and loved. If she cries, her mom holds her tight or gives her a drink of milk, and that makes her feel better.

>**Say:** How does she learn about God?

[Allow for answers.]

>**Say:** Yes, she learns from us. Her mom and dad, and those of us who know her and love her, her friends and neighbors, we teach her about God. We help her understand she is loved, and also that God loves her.

Say: Does this baby know that yet?

[Allow for answers.]

Say: I think you may be right—she is so small, and so young, she does not know God's name yet, does not understand who Jesus is, and does not know about God's love for her. It is our job to teach her. As she keeps getting bigger, we need to do some good things to help her learn. What should we do?

[Allow for answers.]

Say: Yes: we should give her lots of love, treat her gently, keep her safe, be her friends, show her how to do things, help her when she needs help, and teach her who Jesus is and who God is. It is our job. Do you think we can do it? Yes! We want to do a good job for her! We want her to know how much God loves her! Will you help?

Pray: Say these words after I say them.

> O mothering God,
> You give each of us life
> And you use people around us
> To give us care and teaching
> So we will know of your love.
> Help us to share your love with others,
> In Jesus' name, Amen.

12) EPIPHANY VII

God as Our Foundation

Focus Passage: 1 Corinthians 3:10–23

Memory Verse: "…all belong to you, and you belong to Christ, and Christ belongs to God." (1 Corinthians 3:23)

Items for Preparation:
- picture of cupcake with icing and sprinkles (needs three layers)
- real cupcakes with icing and sprinkles, if you're feeling brave!

Background: We'll focus on the idea Paul writes here of building on a foundation. God is the bottom layer, Christ is the next layer, and we rest on Christ as the top layer. Underneath everything, God is our foundation. We rest on Christ.

Children's Sermon:

Say: Paul wrote something very important in his letter to the church people in Corinth. Repeat after me the verse for today: "All belong to you, and you belong to Christ, and Christ belongs to God."

Say: Let's repeat it again together.

Say: Now, look at this picture of a cupcake. How many parts of the cupcake do you see? We have the cake part, the frosting, and the sprinkles. Suppose the cake part is God. Then Christ is the frosting, and we are the sprinkles.

Say: What Paul was saying in his letter is that God is underneath everything. Now I ask you: what if we didn't have the cake part? What if we only had the frosting and sprinkles? How hard would it be to eat that? We would need spoons. It would of course still taste pretty good, but would it be fun to eat just frosting with no cupcake? Would you wish you had a cupcake? Of course you would! Frosting and cupcakes go together. The cupcake holds up the frosting. It just works best that way, doesn't it?

Say: You are getting the idea. Can you think of any other examples of things that go together? Who can help me explain it?

[Allow for answers. We hope that some children will give you more examples.]

Say: Yes. There HAS to be something underneath to hold up everything else. In Paul's letter, he said that we are the sprinkles, Christ is the frosting, and God is the cake.

Say: No! Paul didn't really say that. He did not talk about cupcakes and frosting. But Paul did say that God is the underneath, the beginning, and the start of everything. God is the beginning, and next comes Jesus Christ, and then we rest on Jesus. We can depend on Jesus Christ and on God. We can lean on them. We can stand on them. We belong to Jesus Christ, and Jesus Christ belongs to God, so we are never alone. God is always holding us up. God is always using Jesus Christ to hold us up. Boy, do we need that.

Say: So remember our verse today: "…all belong to us, and we belong to Jesus Christ, and Jesus Christ belongs to God." Remember the right order of things. Remember the next time you eat a cupcake that you rest on Jesus, and Jesus rests on God, and God is under everything.

Pray: Say these words after I say them.

> O powerful God,
> Keep us standing strong
> And teach us we belong to Christ
> And to you, who starts everything,
> In Jesus' name, Amen.

---

13) TRANSFIGURATION SUNDAY

Changing with Jesus

Focus Passage: Psalm 2

Memory Verse: "You are my son, today I have begotten you." (Psalm 2:7)

Items for Preparation:
- text of first stanza of hymn "O Worship the King"
- print the hymn's words on poster board
- sing the words *a capella* or invite a soloist to lead the children in singing

Background: Our focus is the calling of God, which creates the identity of the king. It was the love and calling of God that caused the man Jesus to become the Christ. It is our job to answer God's calling, to find and become what God intends for us, nothing less.

Words very similar to the memory verse appear in the account of Jesus' transfiguration, from Matthew 17:5, "This is my Son, the beloved, with him I am well pleased."

Children's Sermon:

Say: This is the day that we celebrate something that happened to Jesus that amazed his friends Peter, James, and John. It was the day Jesus stopped being his regular self, and became the king. The Bible tells us that Jesus took Peter, James, and John up on a mountain to pray. As Jesus was praying, his face was changed and his clothes became a dazzling white. Suddenly, two men appeared and began talking to Jesus. The two men were Moses and Elijah. Jesus was his normal self one minute, and the next minute he was glowing, and his clothes were shiny, and Moses and Elijah from the Old Testament were standing beside him. It was an exciting thing to see! And what I want to know from you is…how do you think that happened?

[Allow for answers.]

Say: What we believe is that God's love for Jesus is what made it happen; God's love caused Jesus to change. It made him glow. His friends Peter, James, and John could see that Jesus looked different, even though he was the same person. Jesus was changing. God even said out loud how God was changing Jesus. The Bible says that a cloud appeared and covered them. A voice came from the cloud saying, "This is my beloved son; I am pleased with him!"

Say: We'll sing together a special song called a hymn about the way Jesus changed into a king that day. It says some of the same things that are written in Psalm 2. Singing our hymn together will also be our prayer. Listen to the song first, then sing it with me the second time.

O worship the King, all glorious above,
And gratefully sing God's wonderful love,
Our Shield and Defender, the Ancient of Days,
Pavilioned in splendor and girded with praise.
(Words: Robert Grant, 1833)

14) LENT I

Power of God's Love

Focus passage: Luke 4:1–13

Memory Verse: "Jesus said, 'Do not put the Lord your God to the test.'" (Luke 4:12)

Item for preparation:
- cupcake, decorated as outrageously and temptingly as you can get it, inside a bakery see-through box or displayed on a plate

Background: Jesus' period of temptation during his 40 days in the wilderness is difficult for young children to comprehend, but even very young ones understand what it feels like to be tempted. Thinking of Satan not only as "the accuser" but also as "the tempter" is an accurate idea. Giving in to temptation is different from making a mistake—it is giving up a bit of your personal God-given power for a payoff.

Children's Sermon:
[Put the box with the cupcake on a table nearby so that everybody can see it well.]

Say: If you have ever been camping, maybe you have been in a place called a "wilderness." Have you? Do you know how to describe what a wilderness is?

[Allow for answers. If anybody says anything about the cupcake, just ignore it.]

Say: Jesus went into the wilderness alone with God. He had just been baptized by his cousin, John the Baptist. Jesus needed time to think and decide how he was going to obey God and follow what God wanted him to be. He didn't see anyone else, and he didn't eat or drink anything for 40 whole days. When you went camping, you probably took along some good camp food. But the gospel writer Luke says that Jesus didn't do that. He got pretty hungry.

It was just when Jesus was feeling really hungry that the Devil, who is called The Tempter, decided to tempt him. Now, this part of the story is very important. What does it mean to be tempted? Who can explain what that feels like?

[Allow for answers. If anybody says anything about the cupcake, then you have a smart bunch of kids.]

Say: I wonder if you have noticed the cupcake sitting all by itself over there. It sure is lonely. It sure could use a friend to lick all the icing off, and gobble it up. The way we are feeling right now when we look at the cupcake is called "being tempted." We see something we want. It isn't ours, or it isn't for us, or it isn't good for us, and we are not supposed to have it. But we want it! Who can help us say no to that cupcake?

Say: When Jesus was really hungry in the wilderness, and the Devil tempted him, he did not eat the cupcake. He did not give in. He was very strong, because God loved him and was helping him. God was giving him the power to keep from being tempted.

Say: The next time you see something that tempts you, remember that God's love is with you, giving you power. Do what Jesus did, and do not give away any of your power. Your power as a Jesus-follower is worth more than all the cupcakes in the world! Just to show the power we have to follow Jesus, we are going to make that cupcake sit there all by itself and not get eaten.

Pray: Say these words after I say them.

> O powerful God,
> Thank you for giving strength
> To Jesus and to us
> When we are tempted.
> Make us strong followers
> Of Jesus, Amen.

15) LENT II

A Hug from Jesus

Focus passage: Luke 13:31–35

Memory Verse: "Jesus said, 'How often have I desired to gather your children together as a hen gathers her brood under her wings.'" (Luke 13:34)

Items for preparation:
- picture of chicks gathered around a hen
- picture of chicks and hen, with chicks scattered or wandering away

Background: As we draw closer to Holy Week, we can feel Jesus' disappointment that even people close to him did not understand who he was. The ideas in today's passage are too complex for any but the oldest children in your group to grasp. It's difficult for children to comprehend the larger lesson of the gospel writer, that Jesus was seeing the writing on the wall, and knew that following his calling put him in mortal danger. In today's memory verse Jesus is longing for a different outcome—the gospel writer gives us a very easy-to-remember image of mothering love that any child can understand.

Children's Sermon:
[Hold the pictures of the mother hen and chicks for the children to see.]

Say: Maybe you have been to a farm and you've seen real live chickens and baby chicks. As we get closer to Easter, you might even see some on commercials on TV. Mama hens like to swoop their wings over their babies and sweep them along in the direction they need to go. They also snuggle with them to keep them warm, a whole lot like your mama snuggles with you to keep you cozy.

Say: But what's happening in this picture? The mama hen isn't able to get her chicks to mind her. They are running all over the place, scattering away. She swoops her wings to hug them tight, but they don't want to snuggle.

Say: When it was getting near the time for Passover, which was a big festival in the city of Jerusalem, Jesus was getting ready to go. He knew that the king was angry with him, and that the Pharisees and priests in the city disagreed with him. They were not on his side, and they were planning to get him into trouble so that he would be arrested and go to jail. Jesus was hoping that his friends and other people he knew in Jerusalem would be on his side, sort of like this mama hen is hoping her chicks will come snuggle with her. But when you look at the picture, you can see that isn't going to happen. These chicks aren't going to get swooped under her wings.

Say: Jesus was feeling sad that his friends in Jerusalem were not going to help him. He said something that is easy to remember: "I want to hug you tight like a mother hen gathers chicks under her wings." Have you ever imagined Jesus was like a mama hen? Probably not! Are you always going to remember Jesus said he'd like to be like a mother hen? Yes!

Say: Jesus loved his friends, just as God loves each of us. He wanted to hug them tight. As we get close to Easter, when you see hens and baby chicks, remember these words of Jesus, and think of Jesus as a mama hen snuggling you close to him.

Pray: Say these words after I say them.

> O loving God,
> We are your children,
> Your little chicks, your flock.
> Help us to come close to you
> As we get close to Easter.
> In Jesus' name, Amen.

16) LENT III

Second Chances

Focus Passage: Luke 13:6–9

Memory Verse: "Let it alone for one more year…if it bears fruit next year, well and good; but if not, you can cut it down." (Luke 13:8–9)

Items for preparation:
- dead-looking, dried-up plant in a pot
- fig preserves, crackers, napkins (another option is fig-cake cookies) enough for each child; always keep in mind any allergies in your group of children

Background: The passage asks us to reconsider an idea that permeates our intuitive understanding of the way the world is: that people pretty much get what they deserve. Do you think this is true? We tend to tie this idea up with our thoughts about theodicy in general, the question of why bad things happen to good people. Jesus does not answer this question. His response is that we all do wrong, and deserve punishment, but that we all are loved by God, and God's grace is available to us. Jesus would go on from this episode to live out the truth that God does not keep bad stuff from happening. What do you want to teach your kids about this, and how do you want them to understand God's love and grace in light of bad things that happen to them?

Children's Sermon:

    Say: Take a look at my puny, sorry plant. I have had this plant for awhile now. When I bought it, it was lovely. But, alas, it does not bloom anymore. Do you have any plants like this at your houses?

[Let your voice get a little louder and more irritated as you speak.]

    Say: When I look at this pot, it makes me feel bad. It reminds me that I have forgotten to give it water and food, and I feel bad about that. I feel like a pretty poor gardener. I feel like I don't deserve to have this plant if I'm not going to care for it.

[Now get really irritated and mad. Pick up the pot and pretend you're going to throw it. Be careful.]

    Say: And that makes me feel a little irritated. Sometimes, I just want to pick up this old tired houseplant and throw the whole thing out the window! It makes me feel bad about myself! What do you say, should I throw it out? Yes or no?

[Allow for children's responses. We are hoping there will be at least one voice in favor of saving the potted plant. Listen for that. If you hear it, respond to it. If you don't, then you can say it yourself.]

Say: Well, when I look at this plant is does remind me of a parable. Jesus liked to tell stories and parables. The parable Jesus told about the fig tree makes me think that maybe I am being too mean to this plant. Maybe what it needs is for me to treat it well and to give it another chance to bloom and grow, just like the gardener in the parable. Maybe instead of throwing it away, what I can do is give it some water and maybe a bit of plant food. And maybe I should put it in a sunny spot, by a window, where it can get light every day. Maybe there is hope for this sad little plant after all. What do you think about that?

[Allow for answers.]

Say: I like the feeling it gives me when I decide to give a second chance to this little plant. I like the feeling I have when I decide to take good care of it. What a relief! Now I am hopeful that it might bloom and grow after all.

[Share the fig preserves on crackers or fig-cake cookies, giving some to each child.]

Say: Have a bite of these figs, so you can taste how delicious they are. Jesus knew how good they tasted when he told this parable. I am going to take good care of my potted plant this week. Is there something that has disappointed you, and that has made you decide to give up? How can you decide to give it another chance?

Pray: Say these words after I say them.

>Forgiving God,
>Thank you for delicious figs.
>When we eat them, help us remember
>Not to give up
>When we are disappointed.
>Help us to have mercy,
>And to give another chance,
>In Jesus' name, Amen.

17) LENT IV

A Fierce Love

Focus Passage: Luke 15:11–24

Memory Verse: "Let us eat and celebrate, for this son of mine was dead and is alive again; he was lost and is found!" (Luke 15:23–24)

Items for preparation:
- hats, shirts, or headbands for kids to wear, so that you can have a child play the parts: father, prodigal son, fatted calf, and pigs. This can be very simple—make a paper headband and attach a paper cut-out shape of the character and label it with the name.

Background: The prodigal son is a great story to tell in a children's sermon because it is about a child and a parent, and there's no time like now, while they are children, for your children to grasp its meaning.

Children's Sermon:

[As children gather, recruit volunteers for each part. They will act out what you say as you say it, in spontaneous drama.]

Say: We're going to act out the story of the Prodigal Son for everybody to see. Before we start, the word "prodigal" means "somebody who wastes everything and uses it all up." As we tell our story, when you hear me telling what your part says or does, you act that out as I'm saying it.

Say: A long, long time ago, a son went to his dad and said, "Dad, I'm finished growing up. I want to go way out there into the world and live my own life. Give me the money in my bank account—I'm leaving today." His dad said, "Son, I can't keep you at home. Here's your money," and he handed him a big heavy bagful of money. "Be careful. I love you."

The prodigal son replied, "I love you, Dad—goodbye." And he waved goodbye and off he went. He traveled all over the land he lived in. He shook hands with lots of people; he danced every night; he ate a feast for every dinner. And pretty soon he found that his pockets were empty. He had spent all of his money. He didn't have any money left to buy food or pay the bill at a hotel. So the prodigal son walked fast to the house of a wealthy man who was a pig farmer, and said, "I'm broke! I don't have any more money. Can I have a job feeding your pigs?" And the man gave him a job. So he went out to the field where the pigs were and began feeding them with the slop bucket. He threw the pig slop out to them, and those hungry pigs gobbled it up. Boy, they ate like pigs!

The prodigal son started to think that he was feeling hungry, too. "Wow! I'm so hungry I could eat pig slop! I don't have anything to eat! Everybody who works for my dad has good food to eat; they aren't hungry," he thought. "If I were back home, maybe Dad would give me something to eat," he thought. So he finished feeding the pigs, and they got so full that they fell sound asleep, and boy, did those pigs snore.

Then the prodigal son traveled the long, long way back to his dad's home, back through the land he lived in, until he got to the road his dad's house was on. Then he started to run. And while he was still a long way from the house, the dad happened to look down the road, and he thought he saw somebody familiar running toward the house. It was his son, his boy! "Yay, he's back!" cried the dad. "I thought he was gone forever, and here he is!"

The dad started running toward the prodigal son. They ran to each other as fast as they could. They hugged tight. The dad was happy to have his son back home. The son said, "Dad, I made a bad mistake. I wasted all my money, and now I don't have anything to eat." The dad said to his farmhand, "Go get the fatted calf, and get the barbecue ready, we're going to have a party! My son was dead, and now he's alive again. He was lost, and now he's found!" And the fatted calf was cooked on the barbecue, and he smelled good while he was cooking, and the dad and the prodigal son partied 'til the pigs came home.

Say: In this story, the father loved the son very much. This is the way that God loves us. Even when we make mistakes, God still love us. Even when we grow up and go away, we will always be loved.

Pray: Say these words after I say them.

> Loving God,
> Thank you for loving us
> Even after we grow up and go away,
> Even after we make mistakes,
> Even when we think we don't need you.
> Thank you for your love,
> In Jesus' name, Amen.

18) LENT V

A Servant Heart

Focus Passage: John 12:1–8

Memory Verse: "You always have the poor with you, but you do not always have me." (John 12:8)

Items for preparation:
- bowl with some water, a cloth and a towel, and some lotion or cream that smells wonderful
- plan to wash the feet of some or all of your gathered children, or to wash the feet of another person in front of them

Background: The practice of washing feet was pretty common in Jesus' day. What Mary did with perfume, people usually did with water, especially for guests. What better way to welcome a weary visitor who has been walking barefoot or in sandals, than to wash and soothe the feet? Washing someone else's feet is a humble task of hospitality and compassion. If you have never done it, try it out on a loved one. Notice the visceral feeling of humility in taking another person's foot into your hands, and in getting your hands dirty to clean another. Notice the unavoidable feeling that you are placing another person into a higher position than yourself, and the servant attitude you take on as you do it.

Children's Sermon:

Say: How many times a day do you hear somebody tell you to wash your hands? We know it's important, especially when colds are going around, or before we eat, to wash our hands. But did you know that in Jesus' time, people washed their feet?

Jesus taught his friends, the disciples, who were the first Jesus-followers, to wash the feet of other people. He wanted them to be loving servants of others, and washing feet was a good way to do that. We are going to wash (*washee's name*) feet now. You probably think this is a funny thing to do in worship! But it is not. People have been washing other people's feet in worship since Jesus' day. Especially Baptists.

[Have the chosen child or adult sit so that you can sit on the floor or kneel in front of him or her. Begin to wash the feet using the cloth dipped in water to rub them all over, then using the towel to dry them off, one foot at a time. Put a little of the smelly lotion in your hands, warm it up, and rub it on each foot. Try to do this without speaking or laughing. Encourage your washee to stay quiet, too. The children will laugh enough on their own, which is okay. When you are finished, give a hug to the washee and tell him or her that you love him or her in the name of Jesus.]

Say: This is what Mary did for Jesus the day he came for supper. She used some very expensive perfumed lotion that smelled really good. Judas thought she was wasting that expensive perfume on Jesus. But she made Jesus happy, because she was a good Jesus-follower, doing for him what he had done for other people. Remember that Jesus said, "Whatever you do for other people, you do for me."

Pray: Say these words after I say them.

> Loving God,
> Show us how
> To love and to serve
> The people near us
> Just like Mary loved and served Jesus,
> In his name, Amen.

19) PALM SUNDAY

A Humble King

Focus Passage: Luke 19:28–40

Memory Verse: "Blessed is the king who comes in the name of the Lord!" (Luke 19:38)

Items for preparation:
- pictures of famous people your children like and will know, such as the characters from Disney, the president, book characters like Harry Potter, singers, etc.; display these on a piece of poster board
- pictures of the sort of vehicles these people usually ride in, such as limousines, jets, expensive sports cars, etc.; display these on another poster board

- picture of a donkey, or a stuffed Eeyore
- one stone, about the size of a brick

Background: We focus here on the distinction between the lavish display of a king riding into a city in a chariot or on a fine horse, and the humility of Jesus on a donkey.

Children's Sermon:

Say: Have you ever been to a concert or show, and seen somebody who is very famous and rich? Maybe someone like the people in these pictures?

[Hold up your poster of famous people. Allow for answers. Be ye kind to little ones who are thrilled to see Elmo on Ice as a big superstar.]

Say: Is it easy to get close to the famous person? Why not?

[Allow for answers.]

Say: Because we are not the only one who wants to get close to them, are we? Lots and lots of other people want to do that too, and there is a big crowd around them. That's one reason they have to ride around in cars like these.

[Hold up your poster with the fancy vehicles.]

Say: It's much better to be a not-famous person, like we are right now. We can ride where we want to go in our regular cars, or take the bus or the train, and nobody will bother us. But famous people can't do that. If Elmo or Cinderella or Harry Potter got on a bus, the people around them would try so hard to get close or sit beside them that the bus would not be able to move!

Say: Also, famous people usually have some extra money, so they can afford to get limousines, ride on jets, and have fancy cars, when most regular people have regular cars.

Say: This is what happened on Palm Sunday, the day Jesus came into Jerusalem. It was the weekend of the Passover celebration, and it was like Super Bowl weekend, or New Year's Eve in New York City. People were everywhere! People noticed he was coming. But Jesus didn't ride into the city like a rich, famous person. He rode in on a little donkey. [Hold up Eyeore or the donkey photo.]

Say: Jesus wasn't trying to be a big deal. But his disciples, and other people who had met Jesus, and whom he had healed, were excited he was there. They cheered, and the gospel says this is what they said. Repeat it after me: "Blessed is the king who comes in the name of the Lord!"

[Repeat that again two or three times, as a chant.]

Say: We remember today that morning long ago when Jesus rode a donkey into Jerusalem. It is called "The Triumphal Entry." Say that after me, too: "The Triumphal Entry." That means it was a big deal. Something big was getting ready to happen. This week we will find out what it was.

Pray: Say these words after I say them.

> Loving God,
> You always want to get close to us.
> Help us remember you love us
> Regular people,
> And blessed is the king
> Who comes in the name of the Lord, Amen.

20) EASTER SUNDAY

The Best News Ever

Focus Passage: John 20:1–18

Memory Verse: "Mary Magdalene went and announced to the disciples, 'I have seen the Lord!'" (John 20:18)

Items for preparation:
- Easter egg candy, two for each child
- bells and whistles, party horns, noisemakers

Background: Easter, or Resurrection Sunday, is the holiest and most important feast day in the Christian calendar, more important than Christmas Day. In our modern society, we have surrounded the day for children with expectations of candy and new outfits. We do this to communicate to them in a currency and language they understand that they should learn to be excited about Easter. We can use worship time to help them understand the meaning of resurrection, which is more complex than they might comprehend.

Children's Sermon:

Say: Happy Easter! It's the best day of the whole year! Woo-hoo! Let's celebrate! Let's do the happy dance!

[Pass out some noisemakers, and have kids stand up and dance around, making noise, yelling, generally making fools of yourselves.]

Say: It's hard to sit down and be still on such a happy day. Why are we so happy today?

[Allow for answers. Expect to get kid-sized answers like the Easter bunny, new dresses, big food ahead at dinner, picnics, etc. But maybe some will also say the real reason for Easter.]

Say: What do you think is the best good news there could possibly be? Think for a minute. Though candy is good, and spring is wonderful, and family celebrations are fun, think what you would say if somebody asked you what the best news in the world is. What would you answer?

[Allow for answers.]

Say: That sounds like good news. A snow day with no school! A week at Disney World! A basket full of candy! But the best good news there ever has been in the whole world is this: Jesus lives. If we never had any more good news except that, it would be enough. On the day that Mary went to the grave where Jesus was buried, she found that it was empty. Jesus wasn't dead in his grave. Jesus was alive! She got excited. She ran and told the Jesus-followers.

Say: Remember today as you celebrate Easter that the most important thing about today is…Jesus lives! Jesus will always live. And so will we!

[Pass out the Easter egg candy.]

Say: Enjoy your Easter candy. You can eat one piece and give the other piece to someone special. When you give the candy to someone special, whisper to them the good news: Jesus lives.

Pray: Say these words as I say them.
  Loving God,
  We feel excited
  Because Jesus lives.

Thank you for this good news,
And help us to pass the word,
In Jesus' name, Amen.

---

21) EASTER II

Love without Seeing

Focus Passage: 1 Peter 1:3–9

Memory Verse: "Although you have not seen him, you love him." (1 Peter 1:8)

Items for Preparation:
- photo frames of different sizes, with colored paper inside the frames, but nothing else; these should be "pictures" of blankness

Background: We build on the lesson from last week, the exciting news that Jesus lives. We'll go further with children's understanding of why Jesus is unique, why Jesus is centrally important, where Jesus is now, and how we know Jesus lives.

Children's Sermon:

[Display your photo frames so that children and congregation can see what is in them.]

Say: Take a good look at my pictures. I always keep pictures of the people I love most. Do you have any pictures of people you love? You probably do. Where do you keep your pictures? In your room? On the computer? On the fridge?

[Allow for answers.]

Say: Whose pictures do you keep?

[Allow for answers.]

Say: Well, who do you see in these pictures? Who's in these photos?

[Allow for answers. Some good answers are like this: "I see a picture of a cow eating grass. Where is the cow? She walked over to the next hill. Where is the grass? The cow already ate it." Go wild—get silly.]

Say: The pictures don't have faces in them. There is someone very important to you and to me, and we don't have a picture of him. We don't have any photos. We really don't have a very good idea about what he might have looked like, except that he probably had dark skin, dark hair, a beard, brown eyes, and maybe a sort of skinny body.

Say: This is a person we all love very much. Even though we have never seen him, we love him. Even though I am really, really old, I was not alive while he was alive, and I never saw him. But I love him. All the people in this room right now love him.

[Turn to address the congregation, and say to them: Am I right? Do you love this person I'm talking about? We hope they'll yell "yeah."]

Say: Our whole church meets here every Sunday because of this person. We follow the lessons he taught, and we listen to stories about his life, and we try to do the things he leads us to do, but we have never laid eyes on him! We have never seen him. We don't have any photos of him to put into our picture frames! But we love him! Do you know who he is?

[Allow for answers. We hope they'll fairly be yelling at you now. Your work here is done.]

Say: Yes! Peter wrote this in his letter: "Though we have not seen Jesus, we love him." He wrote that to people just like us. We have never seen Jesus, but we know Jesus is alive in each of us. We know Jesus is here among us. We can't see Jesus, but we follow Jesus and we hope to be good Jesus-followers. It doesn't matter if our pictures don't show his face. We know Jesus anyway, don't we?

Pray: Say these words after I say them.

> O, invisible God,
> We can't see you with our eyes,
> And we haven't seen Jesus.
> But we feel your love,
> We feel your power,
> We feel you giving us life and strength.
> Help us to follow you,
> Through Jesus Christ our Risen Lord, Amen.

22) EASTER III

Love from the Heart

Focus Passage: 1 Peter 1:13–25

Memory Verse: "Love one another deeply from the heart." (1 Peter 1:22)

Items for Preparation:
- Monopoly game houses and hotels
- Monopoly board or poster with a "neighborhood" of streets on which you can place your houses and hotels; name the street with all the houses on it "Sharing Street;" name the street with only one house "Bleak Street"

Background: Our lessons from 1 Peter need to be drawn narrowly for children; the idea today is that God created us to live in community with one another, not isolated or alone. We can use Monopoly houses and hotels to illustrate community; focus on this idea of wanting to be part of a body, and of loving deeply as opposed to toleration or isolation.

Children's Sermon:
[Place one of the houses off by itself, alone down a "Bleak Street." Place some other houses grouped together down another named "Sharing Street." Put these into place as you begin.]

> **Say:** The writer of Peter's letter wanted his readers to know how to be good Jesus-followers. He gave many important instructions to them: to obey, to be disciplined, to prepare their minds, to be holy, to trust God, and to hear the good news. Of all the things Peter wrote to them, there is one very important instruction he gave that we can see from these houses here.

> **Say:** Imagine for a minute that you were a tiny little mini-person, and you lived in one of these tiny little mini-houses. Of all the ones you see in this beautiful tiny little mini-neighborhood, which house would you like best? Why?

[Allow for answers.]

> **Say:** I'm thinking that I would want to live in one of the houses over here, on Sharing Street, which are close to the other houses.

[Point to the grouping of houses.]

Say: I'm thinking I would *not really* want to live all the way out here in this one little house all by itself down Bleak Street over here.

[Point to the single house.]

Say: Do you know why I'd rather live over here with all the other people in the other houses on Sharing Street? It's because of love. It's because I want to live with other people around me, not way far off in the distance where I'd have to yell really loud for anybody to even hear me. It's because of love, because I want to see people I like to be around, who are my friends, and not be stuck out in the middle of nowhere all by myself.

Say: It's because of love, the love I feel for the people close to me, and the love they feel for me, which makes me want to take good care of them, and makes me feel that they will take good care of me. It's because of love, and how much I want to be with my friends, and how lonely I'd feel all by myself without them.

Say: Peter wrote about this love in his letter; he said, "Love each other deeply from the heart," which means Peter knew the reason I'd want to live on Sharing Street. Peter wrote that loving each other deeply is one of the most important instructions for being a Jesus-follower. So think now about how you are doing what Peter wrote. How do you show your love for other people? Who do you want to be close to because of love?

[Now point again to the lonely house on Bleak Street.]

Say: And who do we know that is stuck out in the middle of nowhere, who needs someone to find them, and show love to them? How can we love that person deeply from our hearts, just as Peter wrote about in his letter?

Pray: Say these words after I say them.

> O loving God,
> Help us hear the words of Peter
> Help us show love deeply
> To people close to us
> And to lonely people who need your love
> In Jesus' name, Amen.

23) EASTER IV

Help for Our Hurts

Focus Passage: 1 Peter 2:11–25

Memory Verse: "By his wounds you have been healed." (1 Peter 2:24)

Items for Preparation:
- adhesive bandages in fun colors or patterns, enough for each child to get one

Background: All children everywhere have suffered in some way, even the luckiest ones. The kids in front of you can each understand immediately what it is to hurt, and how important it is that God understands our hurting. Children need adults around them who understand and hear their suffering. (This lesson also works well on Mother's Day.) We'll focus on children's understanding that God knows when we are hurting, and God loves us and cares about our suffering.

Children's Sermon:

Say: We all have special people in our lives. They are special because of their love for us, because they care about us, because they care about what happens to us, and because when we are hurting, we go straight to them. We know they will help us feel better. Can you think of someone like that in your life?

[Allow for answers. Begin passing out a bandage to each child.]

Say: Peter wrote in his letter about the love God has for each of us, which is like the love a mother or father has for their child. Peter wrote to some of the first Jesus-followers about how hard it is to do the right thing, to make the right choice, to be willing to do hard things to serve God.

Say: So I am wondering about you…have you ever gotten hurt so that you needed a bandage like these? Who has gotten hurt, and what happened to you?

[Allow for answers.]

Say: I am sorry you got hurt. I wish that we never got hurt! I know that all of the parents in this room right now wish more than anything that they could keep us from getting hurt…am I right?

Say: The thing is, there isn't anybody alive who has not gotten hurt. We get hurt in our bodies, and we get hurt in our feelings. We feel many things that don't feel good. They are part of living. Even our parents, who love us very much, won't be able to keep us from getting hurt.

Say: Even God, who loves us the most, knew that we would get hurt. So God decided to do something about that, something even better than giving us a bandage like our parents always do. God knew that God's son, Jesus, would be hurt, too. Peter writes that the hurting that Jesus felt can take away some of our hurting. How can that happen? When you are hurting, what helps you feel better?

[Allow for answers.]

Say: Sometimes when we're hurting, we need a bandage. Sometimes we need to go to bed with a warm blanket. Sometimes we need stitches. Sometimes we need medicine. All these things can help us.

Say: But most of all, when we are hurting, we want somebody ELSE to understand how we feel. We go to our moms, dads, or someone special because we know they love us, and they will understand. In Peter's letter, he writes that God always understands how we feel. God's love for us is so big, there is not a way we can hurt that God does not understand. God sent Jesus to make sure we know that. So when you are hurting and need to feel better, you can find your parents or another adult, and you can also tell God. God's love for us is what helps us get better.

Pray: Say these words after I say them.

> O loving God,
> We need to know
> That when we get hurt
> You care enough to help us.
> Let your love make us better,
> And let Jesus' love bring us healing,
> Amen.

24) EASTER V

Building on Jesus

Focus Passage: 1 Peter 2:1–10

Memory Verse: "The stone the builders rejected has become the cornerstone." (1 Peter 2:7)

Items for Preparation:
- wooden building blocks or blocks from a Jenga game; one block for each child and extras for the foundation
- one block that is a different color from the rest, or put Jesus' name on it
- photo of your church's cornerstone, or the marker of its foundation

Background: We will focus on Jesus as the cornerstone or foundation of our lives. Before the children's sermon begins, place the "Jesus block" on a table or the floor, where it is visible. The children will help you build a tower with the blocks. You want this tower to stand, so make the foundation layer several blocks wide.

Children's Sermon:
[Place your "cornerstone" or "Jesus" block on a table or the floor.]

> **Say:** The writer of Peter's letter talked about Jesus as if people had decided he was not needed. That's what happened to Jesus—the people in Jerusalem at Passover decided he was not needed. This might sound like a very silly idea to you and me. We know that Jesus is always needed! Jesus is needed at the beginning of everything we do.

> **Say:** The readers of Peter's letter understood what Peter meant when he wrote that Jesus is a cornerstone. Everything we build has a cornerstone, like this one right here.

[Point to your first foundation block.]

> **Say:** This church building has a cornerstone—because before the cornerstone, there is just…dirt!

[Show photo of your church's cornerstone.]

> **Say:** You gotta start with something! There has to be a first stone, a number one stone, the first building block we put down, to start every building. If we want to build a tower now, what do we do?

[Allow for answers.]

Say: That's right, we have to add stones to the cornerstone, to put more blocks or stones beside and on top of that one. Just like this.

[Now add some blocks to your cornerstone to form a firm foundation.]

Say: We can each add a stone to the tower, and we can build it into something tall and wonderful.

[Let each child add his or her block to the structure in turn. Add some more, until you have a nice tower in front of you.]

Say: Now look at our tower! It's nice and big. But what started it?

[Point to the corner of the base of your tower. Allow for answers.]

Say: What would happen now if we took out that cornerstone?

[Allow for answers. Hold on to your tower. Keep it in place.]

Say: That's right, the tower won't stand without the cornerstone. It would fall. So we aren't going to take it away! Peter's letter reminds us that Jesus is the thing that we build on. Jesus is the cornerstone. Jesus is the start for everything we make. Without Jesus, we will fall, too.

Pray: Say these words after I say them.

> O strong and loving God,
> We ask you to help us grow
> With Jesus as our beginning
> So that we always stand on him
> Our whole lives long,
> In Jesus' name we pray, Amen.

25) EASTER VI

Following in Baptism

Focus Passage: 1 Peter 3:13–22

Memory Verse: "Baptism, which this prefigured, now saves you." (1 Peter 3:21)

Items for Preparation:
- one or two Barbie dolls or similarly-sized dolls, dressed in bathing suits or pajamas (or action figures); one will represent a person being baptized and one will represent a minister
- clear plastic storage box, half filled with water
- hand towels or paper towels; beach towel on which to place the plastic box
- consider asking a helper to assist with the "baptism"

Background: The writer of Peter's letter makes reference to Noah, whose story of surviving the flood is taken as a metaphor for our act in baptism, that we are "buried with Christ" and "risen to walk in a new way of life." This part of Peter's letter is a good opportunity to teach children the significance of baptism, and we can use dolls to act out what baptism is. Make sure you incorporate into your children's sermon the particular ways baptism is observed in your own church; if people walk in at certain times, from certain directions, or wear particular things, or do or say particular things, then let this be reflected in your portrayal of baptism.

Children's Sermon:

Say: There's a special thing that happens to us when we are Jesus-followers. When we decide that we believe Jesus is our Savior, that we believe in Jesus' death on Good Friday and being raised on Easter Sunday, the church we are part of celebrates our belief in Jesus, which is called a "profession of faith."

Say: I have brought two friends today [show the dolls or action figures and give them names] and we are going to pretend that Imogene has decided to become a Jesus-follower.

[Hold one doll up so he or she is "standing" by the basin of water, as a child would in your own church.]

Say: Imogene has decided for herself that she believes in Jesus, and she wants to be baptized. Say that word after me, "baptize." We wait for a person to decide he or she wants to be baptized. This is called "believer's baptism." When a person is baptized, the minister in the church stands beside him or her in the water of the baptismal pool, sort of like this one.

[Now let your doll walk into the water, along with the minister doll. You can name that doll after your real minister. Let the minister doll lead the baptism candidate. Walk, walk, walk, walk.]

Say: When Imogene is baptized, there will be water in the baptismal pool, which is called a "baptistery," just like the one we have in our church right over there.

[Point over to your baptistery.]

Say: Now the minister is standing in the water with Imogene. The water is nice and warm like in a bathtub. The minister will hold his or her hand at Imogene's back, like this, and will say "I baptize you, my sister, in the name of the Father, and of the Son, and of the Holy Spirit."

[Now let your dolls act out your description as you go.]

Say: Then the minister will lower Imogene into the water and right back out again. No worries. Imogene doesn't have to do anything; the minister does the work, lowering Imogene all the way under the water, and right back up again. Some people call this "getting dunked!" That's a good name for it, and we Baptists are famous for it! Now the minister will say, "Buried with Christ, we are risen to walk in a new way of life." This makes other people think about whether they want to be Jesus-followers. It makes people who have already been baptized remember their own baptisms. It is a wonderful time.

Say: Jesus' friend and cousin, John the Baptist, baptized Jesus. When we get baptized, we're doing what Jesus did. People who have been baptized say that they feel very close to God. Jesus felt God's Spirit coming down out of heaven, like a dove. Baptized people say they feel like they are a part of the worldwide group of Jesus-followers, the body of Christ. And that feels pretty good.

Now we'll let our baptized doll and minister rest and dry off here on the towel during worship.

Pray: Say these words after I say them.

> O saving God,
> We pray for people everywhere
> Who decide to follow Jesus
> And we pray you will lead us
> To be Jesus-followers,
> To be baptized,
> And to feel your love for us,
> In Jesus' name, Amen.

26) EASTER VII

Strength through Grace

Focus Passage: 1 Peter 5:6–11

Memory Verse: "God of all grace…will himself restore, support, strengthen, and establish you." (1 Peter 5:10)

Items for Preparation:
- list of elderly people in your congregation, or a list of people in your community who need to hear a loving and caring word; print the name and mailing address of each person on an envelope ahead of time
- colored pens or pencils, one for each child
- prepare a written letter on a sheet of 8½" x 11" paper; make enough copies for each child to get one; in the salutation line put the name of one of the people on your list
- Write the following (or something similar) on the letter to be copied:
    Dear (*name*),
    I am thinking about you and want to say hello. I hope some good things will come your way today! I am glad you are part of our church family and I hope to see you soon. May God bless you and make you strong. Your friend,

Background: We can teach a few of the lessons of this section of Peter's letter: love and care for our elders, not to mention *who* our *elders* actually are; our faith that God will strengthen us; and the practice of writing and personally signing letters which can become keepsakes.

Children's Sermon:
[Give a pen to each child, and hold up your envelopes as you talk]

> **Say:** We've been reading a letter that Peter wrote a looooooong time ago to people he loved. Have you ever gotten a letter from somebody who loved you? What was the best letter you ever received? Who was it from? What did it say?

[Allow for answers.]

> **Say:** We are going to do exactly what Peter did. You have a pen, and I have some envelopes with addresses for people we love who would really like to get a letter from us. These people are "VIPs"—who knows what that is?

[Allow for answers.]

Say: A VIP is a "very important person."

[Run your finger through your envelopes and custom-tailor your next remarks to fit your group.]

Say: All these people are very important. Many of them were around when our church got started. Some of them have been Sunday school teachers, choir singers, and mission helpers. Now they are getting older, and have to stay home more, or sometimes they get sick or go to the hospital. But they are still just as important now as they were a long time ago. We call them our "elders," because they are the oldest people we've got. They know how to do so many things, they are wise, and they remember things that happened long ago.

[Give a letter and envelope to each child.]

Say: We're going to do what Peter did, and send a letter to these important people we love. The letter is already written for you; all you have to do is sign your name. Peter signed his letters by saying what he would say in a prayer or blessing. In this first letter, he signed it: "May the God of grace make you strong." So we wrote that in our letter just like Peter did.

Say: Now write your name, and you can also add something else: make an outline of your handprint under your name. Keep your hand very still, and use your pencil to draw around the outline of your hand, like I'm doing. You can take more time after worship to color in your hand, or decorate it with designs. This is a great way to sign a letter, especially when you are writing to your elders.

Say: Now that we've got our letters signed, we need to mail them this week. Let a grown-up help you fold your letter, seal the envelope, and put it in a mailbox. We are still reading the letters that Peter wrote to people he loved. Sending people the message of God's love is one of the most important things we ever do. Just imagine: this week, you won't know it, but someone who is a VIP will receive your letter, open it, and read a message of God's love from you. Peter would be very happy about that.

Pray: Say these words after I say them.
    O God of grace,
    God of the young and of the old,

God of babies and grandparents,
Make us strong,
And let us find ways
To send messages of your love,
In Jesus' name, Amen.

27) PENTECOST SUNDAY

The Spirit Inside Us

Focus Passage: Psalm 104:24–35

Memory Verse: "The earth is full of your creatures." (Psalm 104:24)

Items for preparation:
- light bulb, or maybe two
- large hand mirror, as large as you can comfortably hold up in front of children

Background: Today is celebrated in many churches as the culmination of the Easter season, and the traditional remembrance of the story in Acts 2 of the moving of the Holy Spirit upon those gathered in Jerusalem. Above their heads danced tongues of fire, and they were able to speak in one another's languages and be understood despite their previous inability to do so. When we want to show someone as having a great new idea, we depict him or her with a light bulb over his or her head. This is the flame-over-the-head idea in Acts 2. The people gathered there were all getting the idea that the Spirit of God was with them, upon them, within them, with no boundaries and no limits. The Psalmist who wrote 104 has the same idea, describing that Spirit moving: from creating us, to nurturing us, to enlightening us, to empowering us. We focus today on the awareness of God's Spirit inside us all.

Children's Sermon:
[Hold the standard light bulb over your head for a few seconds and don't say anything.]

Say: What do you think when you see someone with a light bulb over her head? [Allow answers if kids haven't spoken up already.] It means that I have a great idea, doesn't it? You've seen drawings and pictures of people with a light bulb above them.

Say: You have had a lot of great ideas, haven't you? Have you ever had a light bulb appear above your head that other people could see? Well, of course not! Have you ever seen a light bulb appear above the head of somebody else who had a good idea? No way. But those great ideas were inside you just the same.

Say: My great idea today is that there is a Spirit here, inside me, inside you, inside everyone in the room, and inside every person who is a Jesus-follower. If you look at everybody here worshiping in the sanctuary, you can't *see* the Spirit in them, can you? We can't see spirit any more than we can see ideas. But we can still know God's Spirit is here.

[Hold up the mirror and move it slowly along so children can see their own faces.]

Say: The writer of the Psalm today wrote that God's Spirit is what made us. Do you see people God has made? The writer also wrote that God's Spirit is what brings us food and nourishment. Have you eaten something today that grew from God's earth? The writer also says that God's Spirit gives us the power and strength we need to live. Do you have any strength? Show your muscles—let's see your strength. [Flex your arm muscle and show yours.]

Say: The writer also says he will praise God as long as he has breath.

[Hold your mirror close to your face, and blow so that your breath clouds the mirror. Then hold it to the faces of as many children as you have time for.]

Say: How many of you have breath? Let's see it cloud the mirror. The writer of Psalm 104 says to all who have breath: today is the day to praise God, because God's Spirit is inside us.

Pray: Say these words after I say them.

> O Holy God,
> Thank you for sending us
> Your Holy Spirit
> Who lives and breathes
> And moves in us
> To keep us close to you.
> We pray in Jesus' name, Amen.

28) PROPER 1/TRINITY SUNDAY

God's Trinity

Focus Passage: Romans 5:1–5

Memory Verse: "Since we are justified by faith we have peace with God through Jesus." (Romans 5:1)

Items for preparation:
- bag of small marshmallows, fish crackers, or any small candies
- adult who has extended family members in your church, familiar to kids; a person whose parents, children, and maybe siblings are all known to your group of children; you will ask this person to stand up where they are sitting during the children's sermon.

Background: The ideas of reconciliation and justification wrought by God through Christ and the Spirit are too far a reach for children. The understanding that God is present with us in three distinct ways is the liturgical focus today. Many churches will use the Trinity theme on this second Sunday of Pentecost. We need to help children understand this way of knowing God as three in one.

Children's Sermon:

Say: Our memory verse has a very hard word in it—"justified." Say that word after me: "justified." Does anybody know what that means?

[Allow for answers.]

[Give out three marshmallows (or other goodie) to each child, and give five of them to yourself on a plate or table so they are visible.]

Say: "Justified" means to even things out. So, if you have three marshmallows and I have five marshmallows, you are not going to be happy with me, are you? That's right, it's not fair for me to have five if you have three, is it? Nope. To "justify" that, I give you one of my marshmallows so that we will both have four.

[Give one of your marshmallows to a child, and dole out another to every other child.]

Say: Now we each have the same number of marshmallows. You are much happier with me now, aren't you? You feel that things are fair now, don't you?

> **Say:** And I still have plenty of marshmallows. Even though I lost one, I still have as many as anybody else has. This is the idea of the word "justify." It means to make things even out, to find something that is not fair and to make it fair.

[You can eat your marshmallows as you talk, and kids can too. You can put three marshmallows on the table or plate so kids can see them.]

> **Say:** God makes things fair for us, but it's not by giving us marshmallows! It is by giving us Jesus, and by giving us the Holy Spirit. God gave us parts of God's self to even things out. God wanted a way to always be with us, so God sent Jesus and the Holy Spirit to live inside us and help us.

[Ask your enlisted helper to stand.]

> **Say:** You all know Ms. Jeanie (use the name that the children call her). What do you usually call her if you meet her in the hallway?

[Allow for answers, be careful.]

> **You call her Ms. Jeanie, right? She's a friend to you. But she has a mom and dad, and they don't call her that. Who is she to them? What do they call her?**

[Allow for answers.]

> **Say:** They know her as their daughter. They might even have a nickname that they called her when she was a baby. And she also has a husband; what does he call her?

[Allow for answers.]

> **Say:** He calls her by her first name. He probably calls her "honey" sometimes too. And she has children; they don't call her "Ms. Jeanie," do they? Nope. What do they call her?

[Allow answers.]

> **Say:** They say "Mom" or "Mother." She is one person. But there is more than one way that people are connected to her. She is known by more than one name, in more than just one way. This is how we know that God is God, Jesus, and the Holy Spirit, one in three, all at the same time.
>
> **Pray:** Say these words after I say them.
>
> > O Holy God,

You are our maker,
You are our savior,
And you are our comforter.
Let us see you in all your glory,
In Jesus' name, Amen.

---

29) PROPER 2

A Favorite Present

Focus Passage: Genesis 1:1–2:4a

Memory Verse: "In the beginning God created the heavens and the earth." (Genesis 1:1)

Items for Preparation:
- objects or photos of objects that represent parts of Creation; suitable items include: seashell, branch of a flowering shrub, a stone, star Christmas ornament, bottle of water, baby picture or baby doll, flashlight, toy animals, strawberries, pillow, hand mirror

Background: There is way more here than we can take care of in one children's sermon! Let's stick to the idea of our responsibility to care well for the immense gift of Creation we have been given, of which we are a part. Think carefully about your own church family and the theology of creation you plan to impart to children. Start the way you want to finish; begin teaching truth in kid-sized pieces. The story of the beginning never gets old; it is always a chance to build foundational theological understanding with children, who are images of God. You are, too.

Children's Sermon:
[Spread out all your objects so kids can see them.]

Say: Who can tell me the first words in the whole Bible?

[Allow for answers.]

Say: Our Bible starts with the book of Genesis. The first words are the story of how everything began: "In the beginning, God created the heavens and the earth."

Say: Now look around us at all these things we have. They are all things found on earth, and they are all parts of the story of the beginning in the first Bible book, Genesis. There is water, a rock, and a seashell, which remind us of the ocean and dry land; there is a beautiful star; there is a tree branch for all the plants; there are animals; the flashlight reminds us of light; and the pillow represents resting, which the story tells us God did when everything had been created. Which thing do you see here that you like the best?

[Allow for answers, and discuss them a little.]

Say: These represent all things that were made by God, and given to us as gifts. They are presents, for you and me. You've received presents before, haven't you? Of course you have. I'm sure you can think right now of a really great present you have gotten, maybe your favorite present of all time. Think about it right now.

Say: Now, when you got that present, what did you do with it? Did you just decide that it wasn't important, and that you would leave it in the driveway or that you didn't need it or want it and it was okay for your little brother to play with it? Did you put it in a closet and forget you had it, or leave it on the floor and let it get walked all over because, ho hum, you could just get another one any old time?

[Allow for answers.]

Say: Of course not! It was your favorite present! You took good care of it, and you were glad to have it, you spent a lot of time using it, and there is no way you would let your little brother get near it, isn't that right?

Say: The Hebrews, who wrote the book of Genesis, wanted us to read it and understand that God gave us everything we have—all these things, the whole world—as a present. It should be our favorite present! We are to take pleasure in it, enjoy it forever, and take good care of it. The world and everything in it belongs to us, but it also belongs to God. And so do we. God made us to be like God, which is why there's a mirror here. When you see yourself, and all other people, you are seeing a little bit of God-ness. We are part of the present. Let's take good care of what God has made for us.

Pray: Say these words after I say them.

> O holy God,
> You have made every wonderful thing.

Thank you for these good gifts.
Thank you for showing us who you are.
Let us take good and loving care
Of our world and one another,
In Jesus' name, Amen.

30) PROPER 3

Saying No

Focus Passage: Genesis 3:1–19

Memory Verse: "Now the serpent was more crafty than any other wild animal that God had made." (Genesis 3:1)

Items for Preparation
- one nice, juicy, red, shiny, beautiful apple
- hand puppet made from a long green sock
- prepare the hand puppet: place the sock on your non-dominant hand, and pinch the end between your thumb and fingers to make a "mouth;" using a black marker, draw two straight lines where the serpent's closed eyes would be. Also extend the corners of the "mouth" so that it appears the serpent is smiling when its mouth is closed. If you have a bit of red felt or fabric, you can cut a long forked tongue to glue or stitch inside the mouth.

Background: We'll focus on the sense of temptation, which is embedded within each of us, and the responsibility we have to confront the serpents of temptation we encounter. Practice using your serpent hand puppet; get familiar with moving your hand and arm gracefully so that you can slink that sneaky snake around children's shoulders to whisper in their ears, and plan to dart back and forth as you present your sermon, tickle them, surprise them, and make them laugh at you.

Children's Sermon:
[As children are getting settled, don your serpent puppet and allow him to reach around your crooked arm and pop up to look at them. Point his face in the direction of a few different kids. Turn the head as if he is cocking it trying to get a better view of them. Have a little fun.]

Say: The story from Genesis tells us the serpent was the craftiest creature the Lord God had made. He knew that if he slithered up to Eve, the woman God made, he could talk to her and make her change her mind about obeying God.

[Keep on slinking around as you speak. Act out what you are saying.]

Say: God had said to the man and the woman that they could have anything to eat out of the beautiful and delicious garden, except for one thing: what was it?

[Allow for answers. Help kids articulate that it was the fruit of that special Tree of Knowledge.]

Say: Now, it wasn't that God didn't want the man and woman to be smart and to have knowledge. God intends for us to become wise people. But this serpent, he was crafty, and he thought he could get the man and woman to disobey God.

Say: So the serpent slithered up to the woman, and in his slinky and slimy voice, he said to her, "Why, darlin', there ain't nothing wrong with that tree's fruit! It's just delicious! I had some myself just this morning. It's fabulous! You just go right ahead and have all you want, honey—God's not looking."

Say: Now, the woman thought it over for herself, and we must remember that God wants us to think for ourselves. Was it wrong for Eve to think for herself, and use her own judgment? [Allow answers. Keep that serpent slithering along, looking from face to face.]

Say: NOPE! It's okay for us to think and decide. A fancy word for that is "discernment," which means using your own thinking, and understanding, to decide what is right. God wants all of us to use discernment. So what was wrong with what Eve did? [Now hold your arms and hands out beside you in the "I give up" questioning stance, serpent too.]

Say: The wrong thing is that the woman didn't obey God's directions. The man didn't either; they both ate that fruit that God was saving for another time. They listened to that sneaky serpent, instead of remembering what God told them as they used their own discernment. Man, it's easy to let this slinky serpent fool us! What can we do that the woman and man didn't do? [Allow answers. As kids tell you the right ones, let that serpent react by hiding behind your back or under your arm. Let it appear that he feels sheepish, ashamed, and defeated.]

Say: When we hear the slimy voice of this guy in our ears, we can remember what God has asked us to do, and what we know is right as Jesus-followers. We can say to the serpent, "Talk to the hand, get outta my face, go away!" We can remember we belong to God, and God loves us very much, and the serpent, not so much.

Pray: Say these words after I say them.

> O God of joy and knowledge,
> Keep whispering your word to us
> Let us hear your voice clearly
> Let us use our discernment
> To become your wise children,
> In Jesus' name, Amen.

31) PROPER 4

Seeking God

Focus Passage: Isaiah 55:6–13

Memory Verse: "Seek the Lord while he may be found, call upon him while he is near." (Isaiah 55:6)

Items for Preparation:
- binoculars or a spyglass, some 3-D glasses from the movies, or just some obnoxious coke-bottle eye-glasses if you've got them
- prepare to sing a stanza of the hymn "Seek the Lord"; ask your church musician to play it as you sing it together for your closing prayer

Background: Where do you seek God? How do you find God? Is there a "go-to" place for you where you can be sure God is waiting for you? Do you ever have trouble finding God? Have you ever begun to worship, or settled yourself to be present with God, and found yourself bereft, alone, and empty instead? Well then, congratulations! You are qualified to lead this children's sermon.

Children's Sermon:

[Get out your glasses, spectacles, binoculars, or whatever you have.]

Say: I am looking around here, in the sanctuary, because it is Sunday morning, and I came in here today because I wanted to worship God. So I'm looking…

[Use your glasses to look high and low, under the pew, behind the pulpit, inside the offering plate, under the altar, through a stained-glass window, in the flowers, on the top of the head of a bald man who is a good sport or who is a minister—have fun with it! While you're looking, keep talking.]

Say: I'm still looking, and I'm expecting any minute that I will find God. I know God is in here with us, because it's Sunday morning, and we are gathered here to worship God. God is always here! I KNOW God is in here somewhere. Where can I find God?

[After some more looking, stop, slump your shoulders, and frown in a defeated way.]

Say: Does it ever feel like God is very good at playing hide and seek? How does a person find God? What do you do when you want to find God?

[Allow for answers. Some good ones would be to pray, to read or listen to Bible stories, to find a person who loves you and hug them, to sing a hymn, to sit quietly in a private place and be still.]

Say: How do we know God is here in the sanctuary with us right now?

[Allow for answers. Some good answers are that we can feel God near us when we just stop and pay attention; we can see God in the love of the people around us; we can find God working in the lessons that are taught, the songs that are sung, the sermon that is preached, the offering that is given, the respect that we show for others and God.]

Say: Well, you are right: God is here right now!

[Look around a little.]

Say: We can't see God like we can see people, but God is here, and we have come to the sanctuary on worship day in order to find God, and to worship God. The prophet Isaiah said for us to seek the Lord while he may be found, and call upon him while he is near.

Say: There is really no time, and no place, when you can't seek God and call upon God. You can do it anywhere, anytime! You can find God in your room!

You can find God in the backyard! You can find God in the sanctuary and in the bathtub! You can find God at the beach and in the mountains! You can find God all by yourself or gathered here with all these other friends who also want to find God! You can find God in the love you feel in your heart, and in the love other people feel for you.

Say: Isaiah told us to seek the Lord and call upon God while God is near to us. God is always near to us. Let's call upon God right now.

[Sing together the words of the hymn, "Seek the Lord." Let your song be your prayer. If not, use the prayer below.]

Pray/Sing:
> Seek the Lord while he may be found
> Call upon him while he is near;
> Seek the Lord while he may be found
> Call upon him, call upon him while he is near.

32) PROPER 5

The Beginning and the End

Focus Passage: Isaiah 44:6–20

Memory Verse: "I am the first and I am the last; besides me there is no god." (Isaiah 44:6)

Items for Preparation:
- photos or images of Greek gods such as Zeus, Apollo, and Athena, and Babylonian gods such as Marduk, Ishtar, and Ninkasi; be ready to write their names into your alphabet chart
- marker in a color that has not been used to write letters on your posters (red, green, purple)
- poster board with giant English upper-case alphabet on it, A to Z; on the back, copy the upper case letters of the Greek alphabet, Alpha to Omega, with the pronunciations below the letters. (See the following link for an example: https://www.greekboston.com/learn-speak/alphabet-letters-symbols/); leave

space between the rows of letters to write children's names under first letters of their names

Background: The message here is that we can erroneously substitute a lot of other stuff in the unique place that we should reserve for God alone. We can make "gods" out of just about anything we mistakenly attend to in excess, whether that's other people, things, or the gods who were worshiped by Babylonians at the time of Isaiah's writing.

Children's Sermon:

Say: Who knows what an "idol" is?

[Allow for answers.]

Say: That's right—an idol is "a person or thing other than God that you admire or love blindly" and that you give your time and attention to. An idol can also be a picture or statue of a god, like the ones I have here.

[Show the photos of Greek gods. Show your poster on the Greek alphabet side.]

Say: This is the Greek alphabet, and we can write the names of these idols under the letter their names begin with: Zeus, Apollo, Athena, Marduk (use what you have. Make sure to keep the names inside the borders of the alpha and omega.)

Say: Do you think we have any idols today? We don't worship Zeus or Apollo now, but we sure do pay a lot of attention to other people, like singers of our favorite music—can you name any you like best? Or people on TV or in movies—can you name any of them? Or things we really love—can you name some of those things?

[Allow for answers. Turn the poster to the English alphabet and write the names under the letter they begin with, in a color easily visible. Prompt children to give answers if they need your help.]

Say: And we can also feel like we are pretty important, and want to have our way, and to get what we want. We sometimes want people to treat us like idols. We can write our names in here, too.

[Write children's names under their initials.]

Say: During the time when Isaiah was writing his prophecy, the Hebrew people had been taken over by the Babylonian people. The Babylonian people worshiped different gods than the God of Israel, our God. The Babylonian people did not know that there is only one God. They thought there were lots of gods.

Say: So Isaiah told them and the Hebrew people a prophecy, reminding them of the first and second commandments, "I am the Lord your God, you shall have no other gods before me, and you shall not make a statue or picture of me and use it as an idol to worship." Isaiah told them that the Lord said, "I am the first and the last, beside me there is no god."

[Now turn your poster to show the Greek alphabet, and point out the alpha and omega.]

Say: In another book of the Bible, the book of Revelation, God says a thing very like what Isaiah was writing: "I am the alpha and the omega, the beginning and the end." Here is the alpha, the first letter, like our A, and here is the omega, the last letter, like our Z. All the Greek letters come in between them; there is nothing else.

Say: What Isaiah was telling us is that God is the beginning, the end, and everything in between. There is no other God except God. There is no other person or thing that we should worship or love more than we love God. All the things we have written in are each less than God. God made everything that is, and God is the God of everything that is. Everything and everybody exists between the alpha and the omega: God is our God, and everything we can think of belongs to God, including us.

Pray: Say these words after I say them:

> O God who is first and last,
> Alpha and Omega,
> A and Z and everything in between,
> We worship and love you
> We praise you in the highest,
> In Jesus' name, Amen.

33) PROPER 6

Bad Days and Good Days

Focus Passage: Lamentations 3:1–33

Memory Verse: "The Lord is good to those who wait for him." (Lamentations 3:25)

Items for Preparation:
- *Alexander and the Terrible, Horrible, No Good, Very Bad Day* by Judith Viorst; (borrow from a school teacher or find it in your church or local library)

Background: The focus today is on the concept of "lament." We want kids to understand that God is with us on bad days as well as good days. You can choose to read the book if you can allow that much worship time, or you can select a few short passages from it to demonstrate what "lament" means.

Children's Sermon:

Say: The book of Lamentations in the Old Testament is a collection of poems of "lament." That's a fancy word for sadness. What are some other words that mean lament? Sorrow. Grief. Pity. People who are lamenting are sometimes complaining, whining, crying, fussing, wailing, or bemoaning. Lament feels pretty bad, doesn't it?

Say: This is a whole, entire book of the Bible that has nothing but lament in it! Wow! That tells us that lament is pretty important. Now I'm wondering: have you ever had a reason to lament?

[Allow for answers.]

Say: There's another good story about lament. Maybe you've heard the story of Alexander, who had a terrible, horrible, no good, very bad day. Do you remember the stuff that happened to him? [Show the book and allow kids to tell you about it or read some choice passages.]

[Direct your attention to the people in the entire sanctuary now.]

Say: Is there anybody here who has NOT ever lamented? Please raise your hand—anyone?

[And you'll get crickets here.]

Say: God knows that we can't live our whole lives without having terrible, horrible, no good, very bad things happen sometimes. It can feel like God should keep this stuff from happening to us; but instead of doing that, God promises to be with us, to love us, and to help us get through our lament, so we can feel better. God's love is with us all forever, lament or no lament, bad day or good day, happy or sad. And that's good.

Pray: Say these words after I say them.

> O strong and loving God,
> When we are sad and when we are happy,
> When we hurt and when we laugh,
> When things are bad and when they're good,
> You are our God, and we are your children.
> Help us remember your love all the time,
> In Jesus' name, Amen.

34) PROPER 7

Doers vs. Hearers

Focus Passage: James 1:17–27

Memory Verse: "Be doers of the word, and not merely hearers." (James 1:22)

Items for Preparation:
- storytelling hat, Mother Goose outfit, or whatever helps you convey that it's story time

Background: We will use a story Jesus told in Matthew 21:28–31 to illustrate the point made in the book of James that we should be active doers and not just passive hearers of God's Word.

Children's Sermon:

Say: What does it mean to be a doer and not just a hearer?

[Allow for answers.]

Say: There's a story Jesus told in the gospel of Matthew that can help us understand what the writer of the letter of James was trying to say. I'll tell it to you as well as I can remember it. It goes something like this: (use a little storyteller intro here if desired.)

Here comes a story! Oh my dears! Close your mouths! And bend your ears! This is the story of the Two Children Who Were Hearers and Doers.

Say: A daddy had two children, Kid #1 and Kid #2. He went to Kid #1, and said, "My child, I need you to go out to the backyard and clean up all the trash out there, and pick up the dead limbs that fell off the trees in the storm last night, and then mow the grass for me. Okay?" And Kid #1 said, "Naw, Dad, I don't want to do that! I want to go swimming today!" But later on, Kid #1 thought about how much the daddy needed help, so Kid #1 went out in the backyard and got all the work done, even after saying it wasn't going to happen. Kid #1 got sweaty and tired, but had a happy heart and wore a smile knowing the daddy would be pleased. But meanwhile, the daddy went to his second child and he asked Kid #2 to do the same backyard work. And Kid #2 said "Okay, Dad! I'm on it! I'll get it done for you!" But then Kid #2 heard all about the swim party, and got excited to try out the new belly flops he had been practicing, and he put on a bathing suit and went over to the pool, and started jumping off the diving board and having fun, and forgot to do the yard work the daddy had asked him to do.

Say: Now when Jesus had told this story, he asked the same question I will ask you: Which child did what the daddy wanted done, Kid #1 who said no, or Kid #2 who said yes? [Allow for answers.]

Say: So Jesus wanted his friends to understand that it's not just what we hear and what we say. It's what we do that counts. And this is what the writer of James' letter was telling us: be doers, not just hearers. Maybe you can find a way to be a doer this week!

Pray: Say these words after I say them.

> O Mighty God,
> Let our ears hear your words.
> Let our mouths speak your love.
> Let our hands do your good work.
> Let our feet go into all the world,
> In Jesus' name, Amen.

35) PROPER 8

Paths to Jesus

Focus Passage: James 2:1–26

Memory Verse: "I by my works will show you my faith." (James 2:18)

Items for Preparation:
- Candyland or similar game board
- game piece for each child (you could choose to use coins and give the coins as an offering later in the service)
- sticky notes with words or pictures of ways your congregation serves others such as, "mission project," "Habitat build," "soup kitchen," "Bible study," etc. (make them specific to your church)
- sticky note with name of Jesus on it
- place the sticky notes on the game board in place of the other games sites and place the Jesus sticky note at the end point

Background: We'll use the game board to let kids act out the truth we're teaching, that each person takes his or her own path to Jesus. The good deeds done along the way are the steps we take toward Jesus, the revelation to others that we are Jesus-followers, and the exhibition to others of what it means to follow him.

Children's Sermon:
[Place your game board within reach of kids who can sit or kneel on the floor around it, and give each child a game piece.]

>**Say:** We're going to play a game! Place your game pieces on the edge of the game board near you. The object of this game is to visit as many "hot spot" places on the board as you can, and get your game piece to Jesus. Do you see Jesus? Do you see all the "hot spot" places you can visit on your way to him? What are they like?

[Help the children read the words on the sticky notes.]

>**Ask:** Why do you think those "hot spot" places help you get to Jesus?

[Allow for answers.]

>**Say:** Now start moving your game piece around to each hot spot, and then to Jesus. Let's see how many of you can visit each hot spot along the way.

[Encourage kids to move their pieces around the board.]

Say: It looks to me like you are all going in different directions! Nobody is taking the same path to Jesus! I see that one of you visited [name a hot spot here] first, then [name another] but others of you have gone in different ways.

[Take a minute to describe the different hot spots visited by some of the kids. You can ask them why they went the way they went, too.]

Say: Hmm! We are each taking a different path to Jesus!

[Let kids finish the game and get their pieces to Jesus.]

Say: The verse we learned from the book of James says exactly what happened to us in this game! There are different ways to get to Jesus and to follow him. Our paths may take us to [name some of your hot spots here] but each one of us still gets to him. And we can see, by the paths we take, and by the things we do, the ways that get us to Jesus.

Say: Now let's leave all of our game pieces with Jesus, and ask God to bless the things we do, the ways we go, and the offerings we give.

[If you used coins as game pieces, make sure those coins get into the offering plate in a visible way later in your service.]

Pray: Say these words after I say them.

> O Loving God,
> We ask you to bless
> The good work we do,
> The places we visit,
> The offerings we give,
> And the paths we travel
> That you might bring us to Jesus
> In whose name we pray, Amen.

36) PROPER 9

Hurtful or Helpful Words

Focus Passage: James 3:1–12

Memory Verse: "From the same mouth come blessing and cursing." (James 3:10)

Items for Preparation: none needed

Background: We'll talk about words that can hurt and words that can help. Along with the verse from James, we'll teach the third commandment, using our fingers to help kids remember it.

Children's Sermon:

Say: Did you hear the Bible verse from James we learned today? It said, "From the same mouth come blessing and cursing." Now, what does that mean?

[Allow for answers. Be an effective moderator.]

Say: When we say, "cursing," we don't just mean saying bad words. OF COURSE, we do not want to say any bad words! But this verse means more than that. You can just say all the good words, and never say any bad words, and STILL, you can use your words to hurt other people, can't you? How does that happen? [Allow for answers.]

Say: Yes. Even using lovely words, we can still hurt other people, and that always hurts God too, because God loves all people. So there is a handy way we can remember which things are good to say and which things are not good to say. It is part of the Ten Commandments. It is the third commandment. In Exodus, Chapter 20, Moses says all of the Ten Commandments, and the third one is: "You shall not take the name of the Lord your God in vain." That means we will not say God's name unless we are talking to God with love, or talking to each other about God with love. God does not want us to use God's name without love!

Say: Now, hold up your three middle fingers like I'm doing.

[Form your three middle fingers in the way you would gesture to indicate the number 3. Notice that your fingers form the shape of a W. Keep them up.]

Ask: Can you do it with both hands at the same time? Alright!

Say: The way to remember to speak to God and about God with love is to hold up three fingers, and see that they make the letter W. Hey, do yours make a W? Mine do!

[Now turn to the adults in the pews.]

Ask: Hey, can you all hold up your W fingers as we talk about the third commandment?

Say: The third commandment reminds us of a W, and it says for us to "Watch our Words." We should "watch our words," and make sure the words we use are always speaking with love, not meanness. Especially because we love God, and God loves us, we never use mean words to talk to God or about God, and we never use mean words with each other.

Say: So hold up three fingers for the third commandment and remember to watch your words!

Pray: Say these words after I say them.

> O loving God,
> We will watch our words,
> We will obey your commandment,
> So that our mouths will speak
> Only your love and blessing
> As we pray and as we talk
> In Jesus' name, Amen.

---

37) PROPER 10

Wise in God's Love

Focus Passage: James 3:13–4:10

Memory Verse: "Who is wise and understanding among you?" (James 3:13)

Items for Preparation:

- church directory with some marks by pre-selected photos of people your kids will consider wise; you can also bring your tablet pre-loaded with photos of wise people such as Moses, your grandmother, etc.

Background: Wisdom is not the same as book knowledge, degrees of education, years of experience or a straight A report card. What does your congregation consider wisdom to be? Who do you consider wise?

Children's Sermon:
[Display some of your photos. Allow children to identify the people in them, and discuss who these people are, and why they are familiar.]

>**Say:** There is something about all these people that is the same. Can you guess what it is?

[Allow for answers.]

>**Say:** I'm thinking of one particular word from our Bible verse today, and that same word is true for all these people. Which word describes all of them?

[Allow for answers.]

>**Say:** Yes! Each of these people is someone we think is WISE. Now, what I want to know from you is, exactly how do you get to be a wise person? Do you have to go to school to get wise? Do you have to be a doctor or a professor or teacher? Do you have to be old? Do you have to have an important job? Do you have to be a Bible character? Can just anybody become wise? What about you? Do you think that you will be wise one day? Are you wise already? Do you want to be a wise person? What if you make a huge blunder, and really mess up, and make a giant mistake; does that mean you are not going to be able to be wise? Do you think that people who are wise have ever made mistakes themselves, or been wrong sometimes? Do you think that, if we learn lessons from our mistakes, it helps us become wise?

[As you ask these questions, see which ones draw kids' responses and let there be a bit of discussion.]

>**Say:** Our Bible verse asks us to think hard about whom we admire for wisdom. We admire these people in these pictures because they love God very much, and they let God work inside their minds, and their hearts, to help them become wise. They are good models for us. We hope each of you will become like them, and one day, you will be wise Jesus-followers. Let's start being that way right now.

Pray: Say these words after I say them.

> O God of Wisdom,
> Let us lean not
> on our own understanding,
> But let us open our minds
> To your wisdom
> And laws of love
> In Jesus' name, Amen.

38) PROPER 11

Power of Prayer

Focus Passage: James 5:13–20

Memory Verse: "The prayer of the righteous is powerful." (James 5:16)

Items for Preparation:
- daily calendar for each child; you could print next month's calendar, or purchase small pocket notebook calendars (option: display your own calendar)
- crayon or pencil for each child
- large poster board or sheet of butcher paper and a marker, to write a brief prayer composed by children on the spot

Background: We want to teach children to get into a habit of daily prayer, and to feel the wonderful sense of strength that comes in knowing the deep efficacy of praying.

Children's Sermon:
[Hand out the calendars or display your own calendar.]

> **Say:** This is going to be a busy month! Look at all the things that will happen this month. What are some of the things you know you will do in the next few weeks?

[Allow for answers. Go gently with young children who are just learning what a calendar is. Let older children guide your answers. Maybe somebody has a birthday, is going on a trip, has a dad who's having surgery, etc. Name some of these events out loud, and put them on the calendar. Don't forget to include holidays and church events.]

Say: Wow! That's a lot of stuff, and that's all just extra stuff on top of the regular stuff we do every day: going to school, practicing the piano, coming to mission group and Sunday school, going to soccer practice, going to dance lessons. So many things to do!

Say: If we are going to do all these things and do them well, how are we going to follow Jesus at the same time? What do we need to add to our calendars each day to help us be Jesus-followers as we live through all these days ahead?

[Allow for answers.]

Say: Our Bible verse today tells us the answer: that if we are Jesus-followers, a very strong and powerful thing we can do is to pray. Raise your hand if you believe that saying a prayer is a strong and powerful thing to do.

[Don't forget to raise your own hand here.]

Say: Yes! God promises us that God hears our prayers, and is pleased when we take time to talk to God in prayer. There is nothing that we cannot pray about, and this is a strong and powerful way to be good Jesus-followers.

Say: But when are we going to put praying into our calendars?

[Allow for answers.]

Say: The best idea is to plan to say a prayer every day. Look at your calendar, and see all the important things on it each day. When will you put prayer on your calendar today? How about tomorrow? How can you remember to have your prayer time every day?

[Allow for answers.]

Say: Let's write a short prayer we can use during this month—a prayer we can say every day—a prayer which will be strong and powerful, and will help us be good Jesus-followers. What should we say in our prayer? I'll get it started:

[Allow kids to suggest lines of a brief prayer. Encourage them if they are unsure. Here's a sample prayer.]

> O loving God,
> Be close to us each day
> With love and strength
> As we follow Jesus, Amen.

[Write your prayer as it is composed on the giant poster. If you have time, let kids write the prayer on their calendars too.]

Say: Remember, every day we pray, we make the day better. Prayer makes us strong Jesus-followers! When you feel there is nothing else to do, there is always a prayer you can say!

Pray: Say these words after I say them.

[Now repeat the prayer you have composed.]

39) PROPER 12

Picture This!

Focus Passage: 1 Corinthians 12:4–13

Memory Verse: "All the members of the body, though many, are one body." (1 Corinthians 12:12)

Items for Preparation:
- photo of as many of your children gathered together as you can; if every child is not in the photo, just having several of them in there is good enough
- print the photo onto as large a piece of paper as your copier will let you print; cut the photo into large jigsaw puzzle pieces (unusual, no-two-pieces-the-same shapes are best)
- poster board the same size as your photo

Background: Today's lesson focuses on the idea that there are many of us but we are all one body of Christ. We'll use an image of all of us together and demonstrate how we are one by putting together the puzzle.

Children's Sermon:
[Give each child one puzzle piece. Try not to give them their own faces, and give out more than one as needed to get them all allotted. Save a piece from the very middle and don't give it out.]

Say: If you look at what you are holding in your hand, you will see that it is our church's children. Take a good look at the picture you see—that's it; it's our group of children. Can you see it?

[Allow for answers.]

Say: Maybe it's hard to tell just by looking at the piece you have in your hand. Let's put our pieces together and see what we can see.

[Now put down the poster board to use as a base on the floor or a table so that everybody can see, and invite kids to place their pieces. Take a minute to get pieces placed, one by one, and let kids do the work.]

Say: Now do you see our children's group? There it is! Well, almost. Something's missing. It doesn't look quite right yet, does it? What's wrong?

[Allow for answers.]

Say: Paul wrote about this very thing in his letter to the city of Corinth. He wrote that we are all separate parts of one body, the body of Christ. There are many of us, but only one church, and each part is important. If even one part is missing, the church isn't quite all there, is it? Every part is important. Every part is a little different. We can't take the corner part and put it in the middle to make things better. That part has to stay in the corner! No matter how small a part is, or how far over on the side, or what color it is, it is as important to the whole picture as every other part, isn't it? I wish we could figure out where that missing piece is…

Say: Oh, wait! I feel so silly! I have the missing piece right here! What was I thinking? Okay, if we put the last piece into the puzzle, then we have the whole picture. *Now* we can see our church friends! We are the body of Christ together. And guess what? It's even bigger than that picture. All the people in all the churches all over the world—all together, we are the one body of Christ. Why, we don't have enough room on the floor for that whole picture made up of all those pieces! Doesn't it feel good to be part of the picture?

Pray: Say these words after I say them.

> O God of the world,
> There are many of us
> But there is only one YOU.
> Let us see each beautiful person
> As part of the body of Christ,
> Amen.

40) PROPER 13

The Choice for Good

Focus Passage: Ephesians 1:3–14

Memory Verse: "God has made known to us the mystery of God's will." (Ephesians 1:9)

Items for Preparation
- brand new 64-count box of crayons
- index cards, or plain paper, enough for each child to get a piece

Background: We'll focus on the idea of God's will, which is a complex and mysterious concept. Take care in your children's sermon today that you express clearly what Paul is saying, that God's deep love for us causes God to will our inheritance of abundant life through Christ. "Will" may be defined as the asserting of choice, the declaring of a wish, a volition, or a document that tells these things. We've got our work cut out for us teaching this idea to little kids! Though they may struggle to grasp the idea of the will of God or of a person, we can help them understand the idea.

Children's Sermon:

[Hand out a piece of paper to each child, and open up your new crayon box. Ham it up —smell them, pull out your favorite colors and note the funny names, smile with glee. Ask each kid which color they'd like, by holding them up one at a time and handing them out, until you've given everybody a couple of colors.]

> **Say:** Most of you have somebody who takes care of you, is that right? Nobody here is living on their own yet, right? You've got grown-ups you live with, am I right? And the grown-ups have some special ways they expect you to behave, don't they? Now, imagine you are opening up a new box of crayons at your home. What are some of the things the grown-ups in your home would NOT want you to do with those crayons?

[Allow for answers.]

> **Say:** Now I'm wondering—how can you tell what these grown-ups want you to do? What are some of the ways you can tell? [Allow for answers. Some likely ones are that there are rules, or that the grown-ups give commands or

ask for particular behavior. Or maybe they have a look on their faces, or a couple of choice words, or they count to five.]

Say: There is a special word we use for the things the grown-ups want us to do: it is called their "will." That means it is their wish, their choice, the thing they want or don't want, for what we can do. When you are opening a brand new box of crayons, you can choose to do a lot of things! You can draw with different colors all over the wall! You can use a different color to paint each of your baby brother's fingernails! You can take the crayons outside and let them melt all over the sidewalk. You can go crazy with crayons! BUT: Is that what your grown-ups would want you to do with the new box of crayons?

Say: Of course not! No way! That would be ridiculous! Partly because there are rules and partly because your grown-ups have taught you good things to do with crayons and things that are not so good. You know what their *will* is about crayons, don't you? Do you have any questions about the good ways to use crayons and the bad ways?

[Allow for answers.]

Say: Paul was a famous letter writer. He was so famous that lots of his letters are in our Bible. He used his crayons to write letters to the people he loved in many different cities, to tell them about Jesus. Paul wanted people to know that Jesus loves them, so he wrote letters. In one of his letters, which we read today, the one to the city of Ephesus, he said a beautiful thing: that God helped us know what God's will for us is, by sending Jesus to us. Because of Jesus, we know some of God's will: God's will is that we will be loved. God sent Jesus to us, and that's how we can tell God's will: Jesus loves us. Now, you can use your crayons and your paper, and write a letter or draw a picture that shows God's love for us, which is what God wants, what God chooses for us, and what God hopes we will do. God's will is that we will love each other.

Pray: Say these words after I say them.

> O mysterious God,
> Let us know all the ways
> we can do your will.
> Help us obey your law of love
> and let us share your love with others,
> In Jesus' name, Amen.

41) PROPER 14

Family of God

Focus Passage: Ephesians 2:11–22

Memory Verse: "So you are no longer strangers…but members of the household of God." (Ephesians 2:19)

Items for Preparation:
- photo of Baptist World Alliance's World Congress meeting or another similar gathering of people from all over the world
- beautiful example of a cross to display (a necklace, a glass or stone sculpture, a picture or painting, whatever you have)

Background: Today's lesson will focus on the equanimity we enjoy as children of God. We are all brothers and sisters in Jesus Christ, and children are better than adults in their guileless and open attitude toward the acceptance of each person. They can teach us a lesson here.

Children's Sermon:

[Make sure your BWA image and your cross are displayed in a way that all children can see them well. If you have crosses on display in your sanctuary, point them out in the glass windows, on the altar, in the stoles the ministers are wearing, wherever they are.]

>**Say:** The cross is the sign we use to help us remember that Jesus loves us. Do you see crosses here in our sanctuary?

[Allow for answers and let kids point out all the crosses they see. This could take awhile!]

>**Say:** I brought a special cross for you to see. Jesus died on a cross, and since Jesus is alive again, we use the cross to show that death isn't the biggest thing. Life and love are bigger than death. When you see a cross, you can be sure that, somewhere nearby, there are Jesus-followers, people who believe in Jesus, who belong to Jesus, and who want to show their love for Jesus by showing a cross.

>**Say:** Each summer, the Baptist World Alliance holds a big meeting of people from all over the world. Thousands of people all gather in one giant building! All the people there will be different—they will speak different languages,

wear different clothes, have homes in different countries, eat different foods, and have different kinds of lives. They will not be the same. But there will be something about them all that is the same. Do you know what that is? What will be the same about every person there? [Allow for answers.]

Say: Yes! They will all be Jesus-followers. They will all understand what the cross sign means. They all believe that Jesus loves them, just like we believe Jesus loves us. We are their sisters and brothers! Did you know that you have sisters and brothers who live all the way on the other side of the world, and who you have never met?

Say: Paul wrote in his letter to Ephesus that those folks are not strangers to us; we aren't strangers to them. We are all friends and members of the same family of God. We are all Jesus-followers together. I can imagine what an exciting time it is at the Baptist World Alliance when thousands of people are all celebrating Jesus together!

Pray: Say these words after I say them.

> O God of the whole world,
> Let the people who gather
> feel your love and follow your will.
> Bless them, show them how to follow Jesus,
> and let us all be your family together,
> In Jesus' name, Amen.

42) PROPER 15

Measuring God's Love

Focus Passage: Ephesians 3:14–21

Memory Verse: "I pray that you may have the power to comprehend…the length and height and depth, and to know the love of Christ that surpasses knowledge." (Ephesians 3:18)

Items for Preparation:
- yardstick or ruler, measuring spoons and cups, thermometer, tape measure, rain gauge, or whatever you have that measures

Background: Unlimited and immeasurable is the love of God through Jesus Christ. We are going to make all the four-year-olds really happy today—their favorite question is "why?" and we're going to say it with them, and let them say it until they are blue in the face today!

Children's Sermon:

Say: I brought all my measuring stuff with me today! We are going to measure how much God loves us. I'm wondering—which of these tools should I use to measure God's love? How can we measure love?

[Allow for answers.]

Say: In the letter Paul wrote to Ephesus, he said he hopes we will understand how deep, and how wide, and how high, and how broad God's full love for us is. So I want to understand it! Help me out. Can I use a yardstick to measure God's love? Why? How many inches of God's love do you have? Why? What about these measuring spoons—how many tablespoons of God's love do we get every day? Why?

[Allow for answers. Go along in this fashion with a few of your measuring tools. Be silly. Make your point by showing that love is not measurable these ways.]

Say: Well, I guess we can't measure God's love, can we? So, how do we know how much God loves us? How do we know what Paul hopes we will know?

[Allow for answers.]

Say: The best way we know how much God loves us is the way we feel inside—it feels fantastic! It feels happy! If feels so good your heart just wants to explode! We know how good it feels to be loved by God, and we also know because God sent Jesus to show us. Jesus shows us God's love. It is so big that it is bigger than anything else in the world.

Say: God's love can't be measured because it's so big. It is more inches than we have on the yardstick.

[Take your yardstick, and throw it away behind you.]

Say: It is more cups than we have in the measuring cup, [and likewise, toss that aside] more degrees than on the thermometer, more than all the rain or all the feet or miles. It is taller than the sky, wider than the ocean, brighter than the sun. God's love for us is so big that we can't even tell how big it is.

Paul hoped we would understand this: God's love is so much that we can't see the end of it! Ah. That much love feels pretty good, doesn't it?

Pray: Say these words after I say them.

> O loving God,
> Your love is too big to measure
> and your love comes to us in Jesus.
> Let us feel it inside us and share it
> without measuring it,
> In Jesus' name, Amen.

43) PROPER 16

Gratitude to God

Focus Passage: Psalm 107

Memory Verse: "O give thanks to the Lord, for he is good; his steadfast love endures forever." (Psalm 107:1)

Items for Preparation:
- thank-you note
- hymnal, in which you have bookmarked a couple of hymns that depict gratitude such as "Now Thank We All Our God" and "Great Is Thy Faithfulness"
- offering envelope
- picture of people hugging; one of a father and child hugging would be great

Background: We'll focus on the feeling of gratitude to God as a very important attitude for worship.

Children's Sermon:
[Display your items as you discuss each one.]

> **Say:** How many different ways have you ever thanked somebody for something? Let's count the ways! Have you ever…sent a thank-you note? When did you send one, and to whom did you send it, and what made you want to thank them?

[Allow answers.]

Say: Have you ever sung a song like these songs in our hymnal?

[Sing a bit of at least a couple different ones kids might find familiar. Or ask a friend to do it for you, or get your church musician to play the tune as you sing the words. Maybe kids can sing along.]

Ask: Why do we sing these songs? To whom do we sing them?

[Allow answers. Show your picture or demonstrate hugging.]

Say: What about doing this? Have you ever hugged somebody because you felt thankful to them? Who was it, and why did you feel thankful?

[Allow answers.]

Say: Have you ever put some offering money into one of these and placed it in the offering plate? AND, have you ever given that gift because you felt thankful to God? What were you thankful for?

[Allow answers.]

Say: There are so many good ways to say "thank you!" It feels good to say "thank you," and to let people and God know that we are grateful. The writer of Psalm 107 wrote that it feels wonderful to be thankful, because when we feel thankful, we know all the goodness of what God gives us. It feels great! How many different ways can you say "thank you" to God this week?

Pray: Say these words after I say them.

> O loving God,
> Thank you for your love,
> which lasts forever.
> Thank you for the life you give us,
> which is everything to us.
> Thank you for being our God.
> In Jesus' name, Amen.

44) PROPER 17

Following the Rules

Focus Passage: Psalm 19

Memory Verse: "Let the words of my mouth and the meditation of my heart be acceptable to you, O Lord." (Psalm 19:14)

Items for Preparation:
- large copy of a red stop sign you can hold up

Background: From an early age, kids usually must learn to follow many different rules. Today we focus on how necessary it is for us to have rules which govern our corporate behavior, uniting us, and how this allows us to glimpse more fully the presence of God within us.

Children's Sermon:

[Hold up the stop sign.]

> **Say:** Who can tell me what this sign means? [Allow for answers.]
>
> **Say:** What are some other rules we must keep? What rules do you need to heed?

[Allow for answers.]

> **Say:** Now I want you to imagine that there is no such thing as a stop sign.

[Throw yours down on the floor and clap your hands to shake the stop sign dust from them.]

> **Ask:** What do you think would happen if, suddenly, all the stop signs were not there?

[Allow for answers.]

> **Say:** We need the stop signs, don't we? When we have to stop, it can feel like we are being kept from where we want to go! But, it's just for a moment. We have rules like stop signs because rules are good for us. The rules, like a stop sign, let us move well around each other, and let us move forward without hurting each other. A stop sign helps us all go in the directions we want to go, and it keeps us from crashing into each other when we are going in opposite

directions! Many times you and I may be going in different directions, but we are still both going the right way for us, aren't we?

Say: The writer of Psalm 19 said that the rules made by God are perfect and beautiful. God's rules let each of us be our best, to be what God made us to be. Following God's rules is the best way to have a rich, full, happy life, to get where we are going, and to become good servants of God. The Psalm writer knew that we all want a happy life, and we all want to be moving close to God.

Say: So we pray together the words from Psalm 19. When you come to a stop sign, or to a rule you feel keeps you from going where you want to go, then, stop! Think about Psalm 19! Remember that God's beautiful and perfect laws, and following the good rules we have, will keep us going in the right direction. That is always toward God, and toward becoming more loving to one another.

Pray: Say these words after I say them:

> O mighty God,
> Show me the right way to go;
> help me follow your rules.
> Let the words of my mouth
> and the feelings of my heart
> be acceptable to you, O Lord,
> Amen.

45) PROPER 18

God's Imagination

Focus Passage: Isaiah 64:1–9

Memory Verse: "We are the clay, and you are our potter; we are all the work of your hand." (Isaiah 64:8)

Items for Preparation:
- play dough or modeling clay for each child (walnut-sized ball); place each ball of dough in a zip-top bag

- handmade pottery to display; maybe something one of your children has made for you, or a piece purchased from a potter

Background: We will focus not on God's anger, but on the image of the potter. This can be a difficult metaphor for children to grasp. Perhaps this week they can take away the image of the creative potter. At least they'll take away a pot.

Children's Sermon:

[Give a zip-top bag of play dough to each child. Encourage them to open the bag and follow your instructions.]

Say: I brought a beautiful piece of pottery with me; I like it because it isn't like the dishes you can buy in a store. It has lumps and bumps, and isn't exactly round, and its colors are deep and uneven. To me, it is a lot prettier than those dishes that are made by a machine and look exactly perfect.

Say: You have a little lump of clay, and you can make anything you want to make. If you keep it in the little bag, it won't dry out, and you can keep making new things with it over and over again. Try right now to make something that looks like my piece of pottery. See if you can get something like this started.

Say: The writer of Isaiah described God like the way you are being now: you are using your imagination, and making something new and different. The writer of Isaiah wrote that "God is our maker, and we are the clay; God is the potter, and we are the work of God's hand." Each one of us is new, and different from everyone else. Each one of us has a little of God's imagination inside us.

Say: Now stop working, and look at your clay. Does it look like my piece of pottery?

[Allow for answers.]

Say: Well, not yet. You need more time to work, and maybe a little more clay. The exciting thing is, you don't know what your piece of clay might become until you try it out and work with it awhile. You never know how wonderful and beautiful, how unusual and unique, how marvelous and lovely your piece of clay might be! You never know what is inside a piece of clay, waiting to come out if it is worked gently in the hands of God.

Say: God is the potter, and we are the clay. You never know what wonderful thing God will make you become; it could be anything. We must wait and see. You can take your clay home with you and see what it can become when you have some more time to shape it.

Pray: Say these words after I say them.

> O creating God,
> mold us and make us
> in your image.
> Keep working on us
> until we become
> what you imagine we can be.
> In Jesus' name, Amen.

46) PROPER 19

Kids in the Kingdom

Focus Passage: Mark 10:1–16

Memory Verse: "Let the little children come to me; do not stop them; for it is to such as these that the kingdom of God belongs." (Mark 10:14)

Items for Preparation:

- hand mirror to hold in front of children

Background: Kids are their own lesson today—a self-serve children's sermon! They are important in and of themselves, and additionally because Jesus uses children as a metaphor for the attitude and mentality that any person can have, which enables inhabitation in the Kingdom. This is your chance to act like a kid. It's okay. Be goofy. Show kids how it's done.

Children's Sermon:

> **Say:** It's a GREAT morning this morning! If you think it's a good day to be alive, stand up, do a little happy dance, and say, "This is the day the Lord has made! We'll be happy in it all day long!"

[Now allow for that to occur, in just as many different and silly ways as your wonderful group of children present to you.]

Say: Okay, that's good, simmer down now. It's also good to be able to just sit quietly, without making any noise or moving. Take a deep breath. Relax. Ah.

[Now hold up your mirror, and move it around so kids can see themselves.]

Say: Jesus liked dancing his happy dance, and also liked just sitting quietly, especially when his friends, the disciples, were with him. But in our story today, Jesus got a little angry with his disciples. Do you know why?

[Allow for answers.]

Say: There were some little kids, who were a lot like you all. If you want to know what they looked like, look in the mirror. The kids were playing around near Jesus. Their dads and moms were bringing them over to Jesus so he could meet them, and be friends. But the disciples tried to stop the dads and moms from bringing their kids to say hello. The disciples said, "Hey, Jesus doesn't have time for kids! He's busy with a lot of important churchy stuff. He's got serious grown up stuff to do. Get out of the way, please. We don't have time for kids. Move along."

Say: Well, what do you think Jesus said when he heard them doing that?

[Allow for answers.]

Say: Yes! Jesus thought that little kids, just like you, [hold up your mirror again] were JUST AS IMPORTANT as grownups. So he told his disciples a thing or two.

Say: Jesus said, "Hey! Why are you trying to keep my little friends away from me? Cut that out! I want ALL the people—not just the grownups—all the people, the teenagers, the school children, the toddlers, even the newborn babies, to be here with me.

Say: Then Jesus got up and did a little happy dance with those kids who came to see him. He laughed out loud, "Hahahahahah!" And then he said, "Life would be terrible if we didn't have little kids around. We would all be sad and boring without them. Having little kids around, getting silly and playing and having fun, why, that's the best way I can think of to know what Heaven feels like. Hahahahahah!"

[Now invite the kids, and maybe adults in the pews as well, to get up and do some dancing again, and let chaos ensue. But just for a minute.]

Say: So remember—Jesus loves all children! Jesus thinks children are just as important as grownups, and most of all, Jesus knew that being a kid was the best way to know how Heaven feels. So, all of us in this church are glad that YOU are HERE with US.

Pray: Say these words after I say them.

> O God of happiness,
> let us feel your love
> for all little kids and grownups,
> and let the feeling of Heaven
> bubble up inside us.
> In Jesus' name, Amen.

47) PROPER 20

Better than Treasure

Focus Passage: Mark 10:17–31

Memory Verse: "…you will have treasure in Heaven, then come, follow me." (Mark 10:21)

Items for Preparation:
- something kids would consider a very fine treasure: a toy or two on the Hot Toy of the Moment list; a $20 bill; maybe a piece of jewelry you have that looks like big bling; a gold coin (one or two items will do)
- offering plate

Background: We have at times misinterpreted the conversation Jesus had with the rich man and his listeners. It's not about some magical property of wealth that keeps us out of eternal life. It's about how emotionally difficult it is for human beings to pay primary attention to their wealth and simultaneously pay primary attention to their spiritual health. We just can't do both. We have to choose, which is just the thing Jesus realized the rich guy couldn't do. So that was what Jesus asked, out of pure love for the guy. What is it that you could never give up? Whatever that is, that is what Jesus would ask of you, out of love. Hmmm…

Children's Sermon:

[Have your treasure displayed. Allow for responses from kids, or questions.]

Say: Jesus talked about giving up the things we treasure so that we can feel how valuable it is to belong to God and to be part of God's Kingdom. It can be confusing to think about it. We all have things we treasure. We all want some good treasures from Santa at Christmas, or in presents on our birthdays. We want to have enough money, and a comfortable home, and nice clothes, and to eat delicious food we like. We all want these things. It is just part of being a person—we like what we like, don't we?

Say: If I asked you to name your most valuable treasure, what would you say?

[Allow for answers.]

Say: Each person in this room has a list of things they treasure. But Jesus wanted us to understand that belonging to God is the best treasure we can possibly have. It is better than any of these things.

[Now put your treasure into the offering plate.]

Say: Jesus helped his friends understand. He said to go and sell our best treasures, and give the money in the offering plate to go to poor people who need it, and then we'd be able to follow Jesus as good disciples. Now, wait just a minute! I don't want to sell my treasure and give away the money! I don't want to lose what I treasure! Do you? No way!

Say: But Jesus was very smart; he knew how to help us understand. When we think about how much we care about our treasure, Jesus is asking us to care about God more. Do you think we can do that? Can we care, not about getting treasures, but about being Jesus-followers?

Say: If Jesus asked you to give up what you treasure most, to sell it, to give that money to the offering…what treasure would that be? Whatever it is, it is not as good as the treasure of belonging to God and following Jesus. Now, imagine that for a minute. Imagine that belonging to God, being a Jesus-follower, is even better than your treasure. Wow! That feels just wonderful.

Pray: Say these words after I say them.

> O Lord of all,
> Heaven and earth are yours,
> and we belong to you.

All we have belongs to you too.
Teach us to treasure the best things:
Love, forgiveness, hope, and each other.
In Jesus' name, Amen.

48) PROPER 21

First and Last

Focus Passage: Mark 10:32–45

Memory Verse: "Whoever wishes to become great among you must be your servant." (Mark 10:43)

Items for Preparation: none needed

Background: We'll line up kids in ABC order, then get them to reverse order. Then we'll tell a story which has become part of church lore to illustrate this idea of the last being first.

Children's Sermon:

Say: Let's stand up and get in line according to the letters of our first names. Everybody with a name beginning with A, come and be in line first!

[Follow this through.]

Say: (to the last kid in line) Hi there, (name of your last alphabetical kid here), so, how's it going today? What's it like, always being the last one in line?

[Allow for this kid's answer.]

Say: (to this last kid) Well, what if I told you we're gonna change this up? Just for today, we are going to do things in the opposite order, ZYX order! So, everybody switch! (Name of your last kid), you go to the front of the line!

[Allow a moment of pandemonium while kids get into a different order.]

Say: NOW (name of the kid formerly known as last), what does this feel like?

[Allow for response.]

Say: Alright! Now we can all sit down.

Say: Here comes a story to help show how good it is when the last one is first and the first one is last. There was a school like your school, and it had a principal, some teachers, and a housekeeper who kept the whole schoolhouse spic-and-span. The principal got paid a lot of money to be the principal. The teachers got paid some money, not as much, to be teachers. Be very kind to your teachers; they are very good people. And last in line was the housekeeper, who got paid only a little bit to do all of the work to clean the whole school every day. The housekeeper worked very hard, but still, he only got paid a little bit of money.

Say: Now one day the housekeeper came to the principal's office and said to her, "Ms. Principal, I am having a struggle. My daughter is ready to go to college, and she is very smart. But I do not have enough money to pay for her to go to college. I will have to stop being the housekeeper, and get a better job that pays more money, or my daughter will not be able to go to college. This makes me sad, because I love this school."

Say: So the principal thought about that. The principal didn't have any children to send to college. So the principal thought, and she thought, and she thought some more. Then she had a brilliant idea, like the idea Jesus said to his friends, that the last shall be first, and that the one who wants to be the leader will be the servant.

Say: The principal said to the housekeeper, "Mr. Housekeeper, why don't you and I trade our money? While you are paying for your daughter to go to college, you can get the money the school pays me, and I will get the money the school pays you. That way, the school will not have to pay any extra money. I will have just enough, and you will have much more, enough to pay for college. Is that a brilliant Jesus-like idea?"

Say: Then the housekeeper smiled and said to the principal, "Why, Ms. Principal, I think that's a wonderful Jesus-like idea. I can keep my job making the school clean, which I like to do. My daughter can go to college. You are a very smart principal."

Say: So that is the way it works when the leader figures out how to be the servant. That's what happens when the last one becomes the first one. That is Jesus' brilliant idea.

Pray: Say these words after I say them.

O God, you who are First and Last,
you who are Alpha and Omega.
Put brilliant ideas in us
as you put them in Jesus
and let us be leaders and servants of all.
In Jesus' name, Amen.

49) PROPER 22/ALL SAINTS DAY

God's Presence

Focus Passage: Exodus 33:12–23

Memory Verse: "My presence will go with you, and I will give you rest." (Exodus 33:14)

Items for Preparation:

- blindfold, which you will put on a brave child who volunteers, or yourself

Background: Moses is one of few biblical figures to have been in the presence of God in a palpable, visible way. One of the most fascinating and wonderful passages is this one in which God makes it clear that God's glory is just too much for people to behold; and God passes by in a way that prevents Moses from seeing God. If your church observes All Saints Day, you can connect the way that Moses felt the presence of God with the way that we feel the presence of all of the saints and believers who have gone before us.

Children's Sermon:

Say: When you are going to sleep in your room at night, how does it make you feel to know your parents are down the hall in their room, close to you? Does it feel good to know you are not alone?

[Allow for answers.]

Say: What do you think it would feel like to be camping out way up on a mountain, all by yourself? Would you have that same safe feeling?

[Allow for answers. Put on your blindfold, or get your volunteer to put it on.]

Say: Moses was up on the mountain by himself, in the presence of God, and God was explaining what was going to happen next, so that Moses could be the leader. Suddenly, Moses got a wonderful, warm, happy feeling. Moses could feel that God was right beside him. Moses did not see God. Moses could just feel God was there. How do you think that would feel?

Say: Now, even though [our friend] can't see, still, we can feel that the presence of God is with us. In this room, many people who love us are here. God's Spirit is present, though we do not see God. God told Moses that this is the way it would be. God said that nobody would see what God looked like. God said, "While my glory passes by I will put you in the cleft of the rock, and will cover you with my hand until I have passed by; then I will take away my hand, and you shall see my back; but my face shall not be seen." These are the words God said to Moses.

Say: While (our friend's name) eyes are covered, I can come and give him or her a hug, or hold hands, or put my arm around his or her shoulders, and he or she will feel I am near, and that I am a loving friend. This is what happened to Moses, the leader of the people of Israel.

Pray: Say these words after I say them:

> O mysterious God,
> You are here with us
> We are here together,
> And we can feel the peace and love
> Which comes with your Spirit.
> Let us feel your presence
> Even when we do not see your face,
> In Jesus' name, Amen.

50) PROPER 23

Make Your Choice

Focus Passage: Joshua 24:1–25

Memory Verse: "As for me and my household, we will serve the Lord." (Joshua 24:15)

Items for Preparation:
- Prepare a list of choices for your children. Some suggestions include: hamburger or hot dog; cake or pie; Spiderman or Batman; cats or dogs; cheese or pepperoni; winter or summer.

Background: We will put several binary choices before kids, and ask them to move quickly to stand in an instant huddle according to the choice they would make. We'll do this quickly, so they'll have fun moving around, and also understand how difficult it can be to make a firm choice in a hurry. After we finish this brief activity, we'll clarify the words of Joshua and the meaning of choosing to belong to, follow, and serve God.

Children's Sermon:

Say: Joshua gave the Israelites a choice. Have you had to make a choice between two different things, and is it hard to decide sometimes?

[Allow for answers.]

Say: We can get a little bit of the same feeling that the Israelites had when Joshua was talking to them. We can make some choices right now. Are you ready? I'm going to give you a choice between two different things, and you get up from where you're sitting and stand on my right side [wave your right hand] or on my left side [wave your left hand], depending on what your favorite is.

[As you speak the choices, make it plain by waving which side you expect kids to come to stand. They are going to move around each time you give a new set of choices. We hope they are running around constantly, to get an idea of the difficulty of constant decisions.]

Say: Here we go: [now begin your series of binary choices here. Go slowly at first. Give everybody time to figure out where they want to stand. You can speed up as you go along. Try to give eight or ten sets of choices.]

Say: Whew! It can be pretty hard to decide between two choices sometimes, can't it? We can all sit down and rest now. When Joshua was talking to the Israelites, he knew it might be hard for them to decide to serve God. Joshua knew that each of us must decide to belong to God and to obey God. Nobody can make you like vanilla instead of chocolate, and nobody can make you love God. You must decide to love God yourself, on your own. It must be your choice.

Say: We hope that you learn how much God loves you, and how good it is to be a Jesus-follower, so that one day you WILL choose to serve God, just as Joshua did. He said, "Choose today who you will serve; as for me and my house, we will serve the Lord." That is always the best choice to make.

Pray: Say these words after I say them.

> O loving God,
> You are the Alpha and the Omega,
> The beginning and the end,
> And you have made all things in between.
> Teach us to make wise choices
> Which will lead us straight to you,
> In Jesus' name, Amen.

51) PROPER 24

All the People

Focus Passage: Acts 10:34–43

Memory Verse: "Everyone who believes in him receives forgiveness." (Acts 10:43)

Items for Preparation:
- world map or globe

Background: Today we focus on the saving act of Jesus, and the belief that anyone who believes Jesus is Lord receives forgiveness and salvation. We believe that every person is capable of hearing the gospel and receiving it, and capable of being moved by the Holy Spirit to believe in Jesus as Lord. We hold that no other third-party agent is needed in order for us to achieve salvation by grace—only God in Christ, and the person.

Children's Sermon:
[Spin your globe around and talk about the different countries of the world. Or hold up your map and point to places familiar to your children. Has your church taken an international mission trip? Point it out, and draw your finger down a line between that place and your church home. Keep a finger on home, and spin around to big world cities like Berlin, Shanghai, Paris, Jerusalem, Johannesburg, and Sydney.]

Say: Do you know how many people live in our country?

[Allow for answers or guesses.]

Say: In the United States, there are about 330 million people. Guess how many live in India? [1.2 billion, enough to make four USAs-full.] How about over here in China? [1.3 billion, even more than India.] Or over here in this little itty-bitty island country of Indonesia? [250 million—getting close to the number in the United States.] And in the whole wide world, if you counted every person, including the ones who are working on the International Space Station, it's more than seven billion people. That's a number seven with nine zeros after it. That's a lot of people!

Say: In the book of Acts, Peter, who was one of the first Jesus-followers, was preaching and teaching, and said that in every country of the world, any person who loves God and does what is right is acceptable to God, which means that any person in any country can be a Jesus-follower and receive forgiveness from God.

Say: Do you know what this means? It means that it is possible, because of Jesus' birth, Jesus' life, Jesus' teaching, and Jesus' being raised on Easter, that every single one of the seven billion people on this globe could become a Jesus-follower, and receive forgiveness, because every single one of us is okay with God. We just have to believe that Jesus is Lord, and God will take us! God accepts us, no matter where we are on earth. It's not just people in our country that God loves. It is all the people of all of the world.

Say: Peter, one of the first Jesus-followers, tells us in his teaching today that there might be seven billion people who are forgiven, and are welcomed by God as Jesus-followers. It is our job to ask God to forgive us, to be willing to forgive other people, to pray that we will understand how to be good Jesus-followers, and to live every day so that other people can see that we are Jesus-followers.

Pray: Say these words after I say them.

> O forgiving God,
> Let us see You in every person,
> And help us live
> So that people can see You in us,
> In Jesus' name, Amen.

52) PROPER 25/CHRIST THE KING

A Gentle King

Focus Passage: John 18:28–38

Memory Verse: "You say that I am a king. For this I was born, and for this I came into the world." (John 18:37)

Items for Preparation:
- selection of silly hats
- selection of work hats and a crown (fireman's hat, construction hardhat, cowboy hat, crown)

Background: Today is Christ the King Sunday. We'll remind kids that Christ is not a typical king in a castle. While Christ is a powerful king, he is also a good and gentle king.

Children's Sermon:
[Don your favorite silly hat.]

Say: Do you have a favorite hat that you like to wear? My hat has fuzzy pink pom-poms that bounce up and down! What does your hat look like?

[Allow for answers.]

>**Say:** Some people wear hats as a part of their jobs and you can tell what kind of job they have by the hat they wear. Let's see if you can tell me who wears these hats.

[Show the fireman's hat, the construction hardhat, and the cowboy hat, discussing each of the jobs that require that headwear.]

[Show the crown.]

>**Say:** Who wears this on their head? Yes, it's a crown for a king, or maybe a queen. When I see a crown like this, I think about a king who might have lived long ago in a castle surrounded by a mote with a drawbridge. And inside the walls of the castle, the king would have had many, many treasures. A king had gold and jewels and all the good stuff! A king like that was an important person because he was the ruler of his country. He had a lot of power and authority.

>**Say:** Today is Christ the King Sunday and that means that we honor Jesus as our King. Today, we remember that Jesus is a powerful king because he is God's Son. But Jesus chose not to use that power to get all the good stuff for himself. Instead, he used it to take care of and love people. Jesus calls himself a shepherd king. Shepherds are gentle and caring. They make sure that their sheep have enough to eat and they keep them safe from harm.

>**Say:** We are thankful that Jesus is a good and gentle king. God wants us to love others in the same kind and gentle way that Jesus loves.

>**Pray:** Say these words after I say them.
>
>>O God, thank you that Christ is our good and gentle king.
>>Help us to love others
>>in the same kind and caring way.
>>In Jesus' name, Amen.

TOPICAL INDEX

Topic	Sermon #
Agreement	8
Bad days	33
Baptism	25
Body of Christ	39
Care for God's world	29
Care for others	52
Children	46
Choosing God	50
Christ as King	52
Cornerstone	24
Creation	29, 45
Discernment	30
Diversity	41
Doers of God's Word	34
Faith without seeing	21
Family of God	41
Following rules	44
Forgiveness	51
God with us	4, 49
God's Kingdom	46
God's plans for us	10, 45
God's presence	49
God's protection	5
God's will	40
Good choices	40, 47, 50
Good news	20
Good works	35
Grace	7
Gratitude	43
Growing in God	11
Healing our hurts	23
Heartfelt love	22
Holy Spirit	10, 27

Topic	Sermon #
Hope	1
Humility	19, 48
Hurtful words	36
Idols	32
Joy	3
Justified	28
Lament	33
Measuring love	42
Mother's Day	23
One true God	32
Our gifts to God	6
Peace	2
Power	48
Prayer	38
Prodigal son	17
Second chances	16
Salvation for all	51
Seeking God	31
Senior adults	26
Servant's heart	18, 48
Strength	26
Strong foundation	12
Super heroes	48
Temptation	14, 30
Transfiguration	13
Treasure	47
Trinity	28
Trust in God	3
Unlimited love	42
Washing feet	18
Wisdom	9, 37

SCRIPTURE INDEX

Scripture	Sermon #	Scripture	Sermon #
Genesis 1:1 - 2:4a	29	1 Corinthians 1:18-31	9
Genesis 3:1-19	30	1 Corinthians 2:1-16	10
Exodus 33:12–23	49	1 Corinthians 3:1-9	11
Joshua 24:1–25	50	1 Corinthians 3:10-23	12
Psalm 2	13	1 Corinthians 12: 4-13	39
Psalm 19	44	Ephesians 1: 3-14	40
Psalm 104: 24-35	27	Ephesians 1:20-21	52
Psalm 107	43	Ephesians 2:11-22	41
Isaiah 2:1-5	1	Ephesians 3:14-21	42
Isaiah 7:10-17	4	James 1:17-27	34
Isaiah 11:1-10	2	James 2:1-26	35
Isaiah 35:1-10	3	James 3:1-12	36
Isaiah 44: 6-20	32	James 3:13–4:10	37
Isaiah 55: 6-13	31	James 5:13-20	38
Isaiah 64:1-9	45	1 Peter 1:3-9	21
Lamentations 3:1-33	33	1 Peter 1:13-25	22
Matthew 2:1-12	6	1 Peter 2:1-10	24
Matthew 2:13-23	5	1 Peter 2:11-25	23
Mark 10:1-16	46	1 Peter 3:13-22	25
Mark 10:17-31	47	1 Peter 5:6-11	26
Mark 10: 32-45	48		
Luke 4:1-13	14		
Luke 13:6-9	16		
Luke 13:31-35	15		
Luke 15:11-24	17		
Luke 19: 28-40	19		
John 12:1-8	18		
John 18:28–38	52		
John 20:1-18	20		
Acts 10:34–43	51		
Romans 5:1-5	28		
1 Corinthians 1:1-9	7		
1 Corinthians 1:10-17	8		

www.ingramcontent.com/pod-product-compliance
Lightning Source LLC
Chambersburg PA
CBHW071008160426
43193CB00012B/1969